Glimpses of

God

Glimpses of

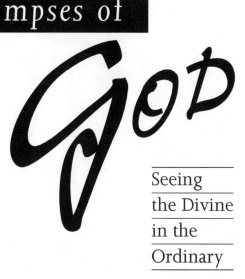

God

Seeing
the Divine
in the
Ordinary

David L. Edwards

Chalice Press
St. Louis, Missouri

Biblical quotations, unless otherwise noted, are from the *New Revised Standard Version Bible*, copyright 1989, Division of Christian Education of the National Council of the Churches of Christ in the USA. Used by permission.

Those quotations marked RSV are from the *Revised Standard Version* of the Bible, copyrighted 1946, 1952, © 1971, 1973.

Those quotations marked TEV are from the *Good News Bible*—Old Testament: Copyright © American Bible Society 1976. New Testament: Copyright © American Bible Society 1966, 1971, 1976. Used by permission.

Cover design: Lynne Condellone
Photograph: Nancy Dawe

10 9 8 7 6 5 4 3 2 1

Library of Congress Cataloging–in–Publication Data

Edwards, David Lawrence.
    Glimpses of God : seeing the divine in the ordinary / by David L. Edwards.
      p. cm.
    ISBN 0-8272-1239-9
    1. Church year meditations. I. Title.
BV30.E38 1995   95-785
242'.3—dc20   CIP

Printed in the United States of America

*To my wife Kaye
and our children Kent and Shelley
and to the memory
of my parents
Barney and Rubye Edwards*

Contents

Preface

These meditations were developed from various sources over a twenty-year span of ministry—sermons, church newsletter articles, essays, and journal entries. In them are reflections upon the glimpses I have caught of God's new life, blossoming gently or erupting jarringly in me and the world around me. As I wrote and compiled these meditations, I did not do so with any consciously imposed themes in mind. However, as they came together, I realized there were certain thematic connections among them and in some cases several appeared to be quite related. I have arranged them with this in mind. Also, I ordered them roughly in correspondence to the liturgical seasons, so that they may be read as weekly meditations, if desired, beginning with Advent.

Our faith gives us a certain perspective or viewpoint through which we see the world and interpret our experiences. This "spiritual sight" is shaped in us by several factors. Scripture, both Hebrew and Christian, informs our spiritual vision. The more we become familiar with Scripture, the keener becomes our vision with regard to God and the new life God creates. So, all of these meditations are in a true sense biblical meditations, for, whether they deal directly with Scripture or not, my own dialogue with the Bible has colored and guided them.

As Scripture comprises one focus of the life of faith, experience in the world itself provides another. Regarding the world as God's creation means taking it seriously, paying attention to what our lives in the world tell and reveal to us. I have tried to look more intently at things, people, events, relationships—in short, at the world around me—as the arena of God's active and creating love.

Our spiritual sight is shaped, also, by community, particularly the faith community of the church. This faith community consists not only of the contemporary church, but the community of faith, Jewish and Christian, through the ages. It is this community that bears witness to the transcendent God who enters into human history and experience to bring about a new order, the realm of God. In and through the church's life, witness, and worship, we gain the language and images of God's new realm. And in the life of the church we come to appreciate and understand the intricacies and struggles of living in that new realm with others, both our brothers and sisters in faith, and those in the family of humanity. Spiritual insight is not a solitary thing, though solitude nourishes it. The deepest insights into life as God created and redeems it are given through the medium of community.

With this last thought in mind, I express appreciation to those congregations I have been privileged to serve through the years: Mt. Moriah Christian Church (Disciples of Christ) in northern Kentucky, a steadfast and loving rural congregation that taught me ministry while I was a student at Lexington Theological Seminary; Antioch Christian Church (Disciples of Christ), Lexington, Kentucky, which challenged and stretched me in the beginning years of my vocation; and First Christian Church (Disciples of Christ), Lynchburg, Virginia, which has afforded me a long ministry with much learning and growth. The sabbatical leave granted me by this congregation during the summer of 1994 made possible the completion of this manuscript. I also wish to thank Lexington Theological Seminary for its hospitality during my sabbatical, affording me use of one of the finest theological libraries in the country and many helpful conversations with faculty members.

I wish to thank Dr. William H. Young, of Lynchburg College, for his helpful critical reading of much of the manuscript. The gentle but insistent prodding of my friend and colleague Dr. William Curwood helped keep the project of a book before me over the years.

I have been blessed by a family that has been and continues to be a channel of God's grace: Barnard P. Edwards, my father, a pastor who carried out his vocation with dignity, integrity, gentleness, and insight; Rubye F. Edwards, my mother, a woman of prayer and inquisitive faith; my sister Carol, gifted poet and spiritual seeker; my sister Sylvia, an insightful and devoted pastor; my brother-in-law Stuart Mill, who brought to our family further riches of ministry. I am most grateful for the life I share with Kaye, my wife, who brings encouragement, love, and a sharp critical eye as a pastor and theologian. And our children, Kent and Shelley, who have enriched our lives immensely.

Advent
Christmas

My Soul Waits

My soul waits for the Lord,
   more than those who watch for the morning....
                                Psalm 130:6

I don't know which is true, that each Advent brings with it more trauma in our world, or that during this season we simply become more attuned to the suffering. Perhaps a little of both. At least I find it so.

I listened to a Public Radio segment on the children of Bosnia. Thousands of children have witnessed incredible brutality—killings, torture, the murders of their families and friends. What will their lives be like, having been indelibly imprinted with such memories? They cry continually, or they are stunned into unchildlike silence. I cannot comprehend the perpetration of such violence. Nothing is ever solved by it. Wars may be won, but the seeds of violence are sown for generations, poisoning the system of the human family.

Advent also comes bringing a keener awareness of personal sufferings closer to home. The double pain of those who are grieving and face the holiday festivities with an acute emptiness inside them. The mental anguish of those who struggle with loneliness or inward fears. The sudden assaults of illness or crisis coming on the threshold of the Christmas celebration.

Year after year, I gain a better understanding of the wisdom of the church in establishing the Advent season as a prelude to Christmas. Today our society leaps right into the celebration of Christmas, a culturally shaped holiday of tinsel and music and nostalgia. Even in the church, there are those who would rather go straight to the sublime strains of "Silent Night, Holy Night" than linger on the more longing tones of "O Come, O Come, Emmanuel." The spirituality of Advent, however, is shaped by the psalmic "waiting for God," experiencing human distress while looking toward the promise of God's help. People who know suffering during these days of Advent are told by everything around them that they are supposed to be happy, celebrative, and joyous. But such superficiality cannot lift us from the real deserts of life.

Advent, by its very waiting nature and message, teaches us not to flee our realities, as painful as they may be at times. For it is into the midst of that very darkness that the light of God is to come. Advent is a season of great darkness and great light. "The light shines in the darkness, and the darkness did not overcome it" (John 1:5). It is the darkness that makes the light salvific. During Advent we learn to embrace the darkness in our lives as the dawning-place of God's light.

Waiting for the light to dawn is not easy. It takes spiritual courage and concentration to watch and wait, to resist escaping into artificial gaiety. But if we are faithful in these things, we will come to Christmas ready to hear the proclamation of faith— God is with us, Emmanuel.

> The people who walked in darkness
>   have seen a great light;
> those who lived in a land of deep darkness—
>   on them light has shined.
>   Isaiah 9:2

Hanukkah and Advent

The LORD is my strength and my might;
God has become my salvation.

Psalm 118:14

The coincidence of Hanukkah (*Chanukah*) and Advent sets me to thinking about these two religious seasons and the common witness of Christianity and Judaism.

In 164 B.C.E., the Maccabees—Mattathias, five sons, and their adherents—took back the Jerusalem temple from the Syrian Greeks, or Seleucids. The fighting continued for years to come. However, the recapture of the temple was a decisive moment in the Jewish struggle for independence. The Hanukkah legend tells that when the Maccabees went to light the temple candelabrum, only enough oil for one day was found. However, the oil miraculously lasted for eight days. Thus the eight-day Hanukkah celebration.

Like any religious holiday, Hanukkah has layers of meaning and themes. The rededication of the temple is remembered. The celebration of religious freedom for Jews is central. Also, the preservation of Judaism in the face of religious oppression through the ages is recalled with thanksgiving. Like our Christmas, Hanukkah contains echoes of midwinter rites, noting the turning of the world from the darkness of winter to the light of spring.

With the destruction of the Jerusalem temple in 70 C.E., temple observance of Hanukkah drew to a close. The observance shifted to the home, taking on the character of a family celebration. This is important. In many Christian churches, the lighting of the Advent candles is being encouraged as a family observance as well as a congregational act. In current American lifestyle, families are frequently pulled apart by hectic schedules, hardly making time for a family meal each day. For many families, other than a hurriedly spoken blessing at meal time, religious faith goes untended for the most part. However, when time is made for a brief scripture reading, a prayer, the lighting of a candle by the children, and the singing of a stanza of an Advent hymn, even that sparse a time devoted to the Holy makes an important, if not saving, impression. An anchor, a center is restored in lives adrift in a turbulent and distracting world.

Part of the Hanukkah ritual includes readings from Psalms 113—118, such as these words:

> All nations surrounded me;
>> in the name of the LORD I cut them off!
> They surrounded me,
>> surrounded me on every side;
>> in the name of the LORD I cut them off!…
> I was pushed hard, so that I was falling,
>> but the LORD helped me.
> The LORD is my strength and my might;
>> God has become my salvation.
>> Psalm 118:10–11, 13–14

There could be hardly a human life to which these words do not apply. Experiences bring us a sense of being "surrounded on every side" and "pushed hard, so that I was falling." But we also experience moments and events of help and strength in the midst of those times. God becomes our salvation, often through the agency of caring friends and family.

At this time of Advent in the Christian year, I find that we share much with the spirit of the Hanukkah celebration of our Jewish brothers and sisters. As Christians, we are aware of the trivializing of the solemn and profound message of Advent/Christmas by the assault of commercialism. In the darkness of this confusion, we, too, light candles, one each Sunday of Advent. The Hanukkah lights remind Jews of their dependence upon God and of God's surprising help. So do the Advent candles remind us of our dependency upon God, the waiting in our lives for God's help, comfort, and truth, and the hope that keeps us living toward the future.

The lights of Hanukkah and Advent survive for Jews and Christians as symbols of hope, of help, of the eternal and one God, who is our life and the life of all people.

Agape and Philanthropy

If you remove the yoke from among you,
    the pointing of the finger, the speaking of evil,
if you offer your food to the hungry
    and satisfy the needs of the afflicted,
then your light shall rise in the darkness
    and your gloom be like the noonday.
Isaiah 58:9b–10

Each year during Advent, the congregation brings food to worship. I am astounded at the outpouring of generosity in the large quantities of food offered for distribution to the poor in our community. The Sunday before Christmas, boxes that have been decorated by our children are filled with the food and delivered about the city to a dozen or more homes. This is a good practice, and it reminds us of the year-round needs of people.

However, I always feel some discomfort about our food-gathering. My uneasiness has to do with the difference between "philanthropy" and *agape*. Philanthropy means giving out of one's "love for humanity"(*phil*—from a Greek word meaning a certain kind of love; *anthropy*—from the word for human beings) Usually, philanthropic giving, though it may be quite generous, comes out of what we have in excess—we give what we don't need, enough so as to be generous, but not so much as to affect our own well-being. *Agape* is not giving out of our own sense of love, but out of God's love in us, which is utterly self-giving.

Philanthropy is based upon our own love of our fellow human beings. This is a shaky foundation for giving. Our human capacity for loving others is notoriously undependable and episodic. We may give to others as long as they do and live as we expect they should. We may give to others as long as we are assured that they are "deserving." Philanthropy is safe love, for its costs us nothing, asks us to take no risks, and lets us be "in charge." *Agape*, however, as the love we know in the biblical witness, is self-giving, risk-taking, all-out giving for others. *Agape* is rooted in God's own all-out love for us and the world. It is *crucified* love.

> *See* what love the Father has given us…In this is love, not that we loved God but that God loved us and sent his Son to be the atoning sacrifice for our sins. Beloved, since God loved us so much, we also ought to love one another.
>
> 1 John 3:1a, 4:10–11

Yet there is another dimension to my reservations about our Christmas food gifts. During the pre-Christmas season there arise many appeals urging us to respond to the needs of people.

Quite often the approach of these philanthropic campaigns has to do with how good we will feel when we give.

We must not discount good feelings that come when we give to others, for they often are telling us that in giving we touch our true selves. This is very important. However, there exists a deeper-lying issue related to the needs of the hungry, the homeless, and all who are deprived in a nation of plenty. The issue is *justice*. One senses that the general public, including the church, often uses the poor or needy in order to stimulate good feelings. This is a subtly self-centered and self-serving structure of giving, certainly not in the tradition of justice expressed in scripture. Isaiah's words convey God's own commands that injustices be corrected in Israel's life so that then God might be known. God's reality and presence are disclosed as justice, mercy, compassion are worked into the structures of human society. Good feelings are one thing. Knowing God is another.

We need to give at this time of year. Our efforts should not be diminished, but redoubled. Every bit truly helps! And yet, we know that our little bit cannot wipe away the conditions that cause poverty in our society and world, or reshape an economy that beats down some and lets others become multi-billionaires, or change the values that tell us it is acceptable for some to earn as much money as they want while others do not have enough. We need to give our Christmas baskets, but as a sign of justice, what God requires, not as an expression of our own generosity or goodness of spirit. As we live more and more out of *agape* and justice, then the light of God's realm will dawn more fully in our own lives and in our world.

The True Christmas Spirit

We want you to know, brothers and sisters, about
the grace of God that has been granted to the
churches of Macedonia; for during a severe
ordeal of affliction, their abundant joy and
their extreme poverty have overflowed in a
wealth of generosity....

2 Corinthians 8:1–2

One Sunday evening I ran into Suzanne in the hallway of
the church. She had come to pick up her children from choir
practice. I could hear the children in the choir room, going
through their pieces for the Christmas Eve service. Their voices
sounded truly "angelic"—no kidding!

I stopped, glad to have a chance to visit with Suzanne. She
is one of my favorite people, for she teaches me a great deal
about faith. Her life has been full of struggles—abuse, unemployment, raising three biracial children in a community still
very racist, having hardly enough money for necessities and none
for luxuries.

Suzanne stumbled upon our church a few years ago. I was
elated when she told me how welcomed she felt. Ours is not a
wealthy church, but we're not poor either. We have a certain
mix of people, economically speaking. Yet it concerns me when
I see how social and economic factors shape the makeup of our
churches more than the gospel itself. To me, it is a gift from
God when someone with a background like Suzanne's finds
warmth and welcome in our largely white middle-class churches.

However, from my perspective, the most important thing is
what Suzanne has brought to the church. She would put it the
other way around. But that is part of her genuine humility.

As we talked, Suzanne filled me in on Christmas preparations at their home. She was recently married to a man she greatly deserves. I felt it a special privilege to share in their marriage. She briefed me on how they were wrestling with what they could and could not get the children this year, mostly what they could not afford. It would be a lean Christmas, gift-wise…but not in terms of love, I thought.

Suzanne then told me that she had just gone by a friend's house to pick up the middle tier of their wedding cake. Since Suzanne has no freezer, her friend had offered to keep it. Suzanne had decided to take the cake to the local soup kitchen. She didn't need it, and those folks would enjoy it, she said.

"You know," she then spoke confessionally, "I've had such a hard time getting the Christmas spirit this year." I think I understood what she was saying. Her life is so full of difficulties and challenges that the lightheartedness of the Christmas season has little to do with the weariness and struggle of her own spirit.

As I drove home later that evening, I thought of what I wish I had said to Suzanne. "You're having difficulty getting the Christmas spirit? You ARE the Christmas spirit!" Later I was able to say this to her. Here is this woman who has so little, shows no jealousy that others have more, is constantly thinking up ways to give to others, spinning gold out of the straw of her material life! What could be more accurately the true Christmas spirit than that? It is the spirit of Christ himself.

What we call the "Christmas spirit" usually is a mix of sentimental and nostalgic feelings, as we gaze mistily at Christmas lights and manger scenes, or sing "White Christmas." Certainly there is a kind of warmth and mellowness that comes with the season, but is not the essence of it. The deeper level of meaning has to do with something far more life-giving.

I see that the church continues to have much work on its hands, rescuing the spiritual dimension of Advent and Christmas from the mire of our cultural distortion of the season. People like Suzanne help us move in the right direction.

I do not propose that we throw out our Christmas songs, our tinsel, and our gaiety. Only that we also learn to sing another song, one that we pray will fill the hearts of all people—Mary's "Christmas song":

"My soul magnifies the Lord,
    and my spirit rejoices in God my Savior,
for he has looked with favor on the lowliness
        of his servant....
God has brought down the powerful
        from their thrones,
    and lifted up the lowly;
God has filled the hungry with good things,
    and sent the rich away empty.
God has helped his servant Israel,
    in remembrance of his mercy...."
                                    Luke 1:46b–48a, 52–54

Our Tears into Dancing

You have turned my mourning into dancing;
    you have taken off my sackcloth
    and clothed me with joy,
so that my soul may praise you
    and not be silent.
O LORD, my God, I will give thanks to
    you forever.

Psalm 30:11–12

Normally, I come to Christmas Eve extremely tired from the extra demands of the season. Yet our two evening services stir in me a sense of anticipation. Over the years, I have begun to learn the dynamic relationship between Advent and Christmas—waiting and fulfillment, preparation and arrival. By Christmas Eve, my own life often feels like the desert in which John shouted out his announcement of the coming of God. I hear the shout, but as yet I don't see God! This is so much a part of the nature of the life of faith—living in trustful expectancy.

Susan has been working with her liturgical dance group all through the fall, preparing Advent and Christmas pieces. From time to time, she has spoken with me about Paula, a young mentally handicapped girl who has become part of the group. Paula's mother had heard of our dance ensemble and approached Susan about her daughter being involved. It was obviously important for her to find some place, some activity like this for her daughter, to whom other such programs were closed. Paula had been turned down elsewhere because she would "slow down" the progress of others and "the program"! It may not have been said in so many words, but the meaning was clear.

This Christmas Eve, the dancers, Paula included, were to be part of our early service, which is mostly for children and older people who cannot come out to the late-night communion service. For the first time I would see Paula dance.

As I watched the dancers, especially Paula, lifting their candles and processing to the congregation's singing of "O Come, O Come, Emmanuel," a tightness gripped my throat and tears stung my eyes. I knew that Susan and the other dancers had worked hard, paying special attention to Paula, guiding her, encouraging her. In a real sense, I think, their movements were shaped around their "slower" member. I knew how difficult it had been, how they, too, had to come to grips with how Paula "slowed them down." The difference was that they perceived this "slowing down" as a gift from God, teaching them something important.

My own spirit had come into this Christmas Eve service heavy and numb from the accumulated weight of pastoral work. Now, suddenly, a light kindled inside of me and the weight was lifted. This is what it is all about! This is the proclamation of Jesus Christ himself! Here is one of the least of his sisters and brothers, in whom we meet God who is with us—Emmanuel!

After the service, I met Paula's grandmother who had come to see her special granddaughter dance. Her face was aglow, eyes glistening with happiness and love. Later, Susan shared what this loving grandmother had said to her, that this was the best Christmas gift she had ever received. I knew what she meant.

Serving God with Gladness

Make a joyful noise to the LORD, all the earth.
Worship the LORD with gladness;
come into God's presence with singing.

Psalm 100:1–2

The Sunday after Christmas is always an enigma for me. I never know what to expect. Worship attendance is down. And I feel a kind of physical, emotional, and spiritual hangover from the pace of Advent and Christmas Eve activities and services. Everything's a little out of kilter, and I approach that Sunday's service without much energy, yet relaxed.

As we sang the communion hymn, I looked up at the two elders and the diaconate members processing down the aisle to serve. There was Keith, right in line. Now, Keith is one of our members who has Down's syndrome. He had been in an energetic mood that morning. My church school class had only a couple of members, who had to leave early for choir rehearsal. Keith likes to visit around the classes, so he dropped in for a chat. After the others drifted off to choir, Keith and I remained to talk. Frequently he interjected with vigor the comment about this being "my church." He said this with much emphasis, expressing his pride that he belonged to this congregation. Since his baptism the previous summer, Keith had taken his faith and the church very seriously.

Our congregation has several mentally handicapped members. People have received them, for the most part, not as objects of pity or even benevolence, but as full members. We have endeavored to see these persons for the special gifts they bring to us. As a result, they have felt accepted and affirmed, and have contributed greatly to the life and work of the congregation.

Keith has been in the forefront in the enthusiasm department! He has always been eager to do anything and everything—lighting the candles for worship, helping with the children, or handing out bulletins. On this particular day, Keith had signed up to provide flowers for the sanctuary one Sunday in the spring. His reading is very minimal, so I smiled as I saw he had put his name on the sign-up sheet, probably not knowing what it was about. I also found myself wishing that all our members were as eager!

So, here came Keith to serve communion! His volunteer spirit had swept him right in line with the diaconate, which was shorthanded that day. Another of our members who is mentally handicapped had been elected to the diaconate the previous year. But Keith had never served communion, though he had been mentioned as a future deacon.

As this situation was evolving, I felt my old penchant for controlling everything kick in. When the elders and diaconate arrived at the communion table, I leaned over to one of the elders, who, fortunately, was a person seldom rattled by such turns of events. I asked her if she would watch out for Keith and give him some guidance if necessary. She nodded consent in a way that calmed me considerably.

When the time came for the elders to hand the communion trays to the diaconate, off went Keith. The elder simply sat down on the bench beside me, as usual, as if to say, "It's going to be all right, whatever happens." We watched to see how the drama would unfold.

Keith walked down the chancel steps, scanned the congregation, momentarily hesitating, then chose his course. He headed off down the side aisle of the nave and took his post at the back to begin serving. During this hesitation, the other diaconate members simply watched Keith to see where he would go, then adjusted themselves accordingly. Everything went smoothly.

It was then that I began to grasp the significance of what was taking place. There was Keith, serving the bread and cup of Christ's supper to his brother and sister believers. He had known nearly exactly what to do! Obviously he had been paying close attention every Sunday to know how this was all done. And when the Spirit moved him, he answered the call and stepped in line.

Communion never meant any more to me, and many others, than that morning when, by God's grace, the sea of our conventionalism and rigidity suddenly parted, and Keith led us through to the promised land. A warm gratefulness washed over me because of this congregation that could make room for this unexpected and exemplary servant of God.

Therefore, my beloved, be steadfast, immovable, always excelling in the work of the Lord....
1 Corinthians 15:58a

Pondering in Our Hearts

But Mary treasured all these words and pondered them in her heart.
Luke 2:19

A few days after Christmas, I took our children to the mall. As we walked about, I finally realized what was different. All the tons of holiday decorations and the omnipresent taped Christmas music that served as a "white noise" for harried shoppers who never looked as though they were enjoying this season of joy—it was all gone! Vanished, without a trace, as though it had never happened. Around Thanksgiving, or before, actually, the commercial paraphernalia crept in like kudzu along southern roads, covering everything with Santa Clauses, puffy cotton, blinking lights, and every imaginable thing. But, in the wink of an eye, it disappeared, as though to say, "Well, we've done Christmas now. On to the next holiday!"

Here is a spiritual dilemma. We "put away" Christmas quickly. Once the presents are opened, it's all over. I remember as a child feeling a depression slowly come over me as Christmas night came, leaving the glitter of Christmas Eve and the excitement of Christmas morning behind. After the big buildup, it was over, and the late hours of Christmas Day became pale and flat.

Some of this after-Christmas Day feeling still lingers for me. Yet, this may be helpful. When the gloss of Christmas celebration has been removed, there is, at last, some emptiness, some quiet, some rest for the eye and spirit. Then we can reflect on what was hidden beneath all the glitter and distractions. We have Advent as a necessary preparation for the Christmas good news of God's incarnation in Jesus Christ. You can't just "jump into" something that profound! Likewise, we have Christmastide in order to reflect more deeply upon what has been proclaimed— "God is with us!"

Our lives become so hurried as we fill our schedules, doing all manner of things. Of course, much of what we do may be very important—raising children, attending meetings, fulfilling sundry obligations. We complain of stress, underneath which we feel a loss of meaning in our lives. Yet, how many significant events, people, words, sights, sounds are part of our lives every day, and we hardly notice? Or, if we notice, we do not have or make the time to let these things "sink in," to let them enrich our lives. We would do well to cultivate, if not more time, at least a greater awareness in our spirits so that we truly *live* our lives rather than "go through" them.

How relieved I felt that evening, walking around the mall with my children in the refreshing quiet and vacancy! At last, time and space to "treasure all these things and ponder them in my heart!"

Epiphany

Under the Night Sky

When I look at your heavens, the work of
  your fingers,
the moon and the stars that you have established;
what are human beings that you are mindful of them,
  mortals that you care for them?

Psalm 8:3–4

Clear, cold December nights are spectacular! The stars are chunks of crystal nestled in the ebony velvet of the sky. In our neighborhood, where street lights are few and far between, the view of the night sky can be breathtaking.

I have been walking more at night in recent years, especially in the winter. I take all the sadness and joy of my life out into the crisp, cold air, and the star-flecked darkness. The bewilderment I may feel about life, I find, needs to be brought under the expanse of night sky. "When I consider the moon and stars...who am I that you should consider me?" I like this expression of awe at both our human smallness, even nothingness, and God's concern and care. The sense of our nothingness—Who are we!—constitutes an important part of our spirits and lives as human beings.

Sensitive and caring persons, we become easily aware of the tremendous and overwhelming needs of people and our world. At times we encounter in ourselves the sense of being utterly powerless to make a difference. What can I do that really matters? Feeling small and powerless is much more than simply a psychological or emotional barrier to be overcome by the exertion of our wills. It is part of who we are, human beings living in a very, very large cosmos!

There are moments when I feel the weight of my struggles with fear, pain, and failure. This constitutes much of my encounter with nothingness. I see in myself, also, a persistent and subtle desire to be recognized for doing important things. And yet, what I do seems so little, so fleeting, and a wisp of pride. This, too, is nothingness.

The book of Ecclesiastes has become a favorite of mine. I've come to read it as a kind of Judeo-Christian existentialist meditation. The writer speaks of "vanity," the experience of the emptiness of so much of life. Vanity in the reflections of Ecclesiastes expresses what the writer finds when he seeks ultimate meaning in the mundane things of life—when, we might say, he expects more of life than life can offer. After the writer has searched through and seen "everything under the sun," and finds that it is all vanity, then he is ready to accept human life as it is—limited, offering rhythms of pain and pleasure, sorrow and joy, emptiness and meaning. And yet, this very life—limited, modest—is God's gift. The writer then finds that his vocation is to be happy in this life.

When I encounter this nothingness, or vanity, in my own life, I take it out under the winter night sky. There my sense of nothingness is answered by the silence of the world, which bestows a particular kind of wholeness upon my spirit. Yes, I *am* nothing. I *am* dust, and to dust I will return. My days *are* like grass—here today, gone tomorrow. Yet, I realize that this nothingness we experience is part of what it means to be a human being, to be a "creature." It does no good to try to fend off the experience; this only intensifies it. When we embrace this part of our created humanity, we discover something close to the true meaning of humility. We see ourselves within the wide expanse of God's universe, but also within the tender care of that same infinite God. Out of our nothingness, we yet are and can be something—not everything—but something.

> So teach us to number our days
> that we may gain a wise heart.
> Psalm 90:12

Dirty Corner Versus Whole Reality

...what are human beings that you are
mindful of them,
mortals that you care for them?

Psalm 8:4

In Richmond for a meeting, I had a couple of free hours. So I headed for the Virginia Museum of Fine Arts. The first exhibit I encountered was a collection of contemporary paintings. Normally, I have a difficult time with such works—ignorant, most likely, about how to approach or appreciate them. At the outset, then, I confess my aesthetic limitations and prejudices.

One painting, however, did grab my attention. It pictured the corner of a presumably empty room, as though someone had just moved out. An assortment of refuse cluttered the floor, paint speckled the molding and radiator, and a frayed light cord hung limply from the wall socket. I was fondly reminded of the places my wife and I inhabited early in our marriage.

As I continued to look at the painting, a mild depression, or boredom, overtook me. The painting was certainly introspective, asking the viewer to stare at a vacant, dirty corner. This is not bad. We do, indeed, live our lives immersed in detail, and we need to pay attention to the mundane world of which we are a part. However tempted, we cannot fly off into an airy spirituality that takes us out of the concrete, everyday world that is ours, including our "dirty corners."

After a while, I extricated myself from the exhibit, feeling a kind of pride for enduring beyond my usual limit. I moved on, making my way quickly to the Oriental exhibit, which had become my favorite in previous visits. As soon as I entered the rooms of Japanese and Chinese works, I felt relief, an opening up of my spirit. The paintings I viewed there were as broad in scope as the "dirty corner" canvas was myopic. Typically, Oriental painting attempts to bring human beings, the world of nature, and even infinity into an artistic whole. Everything, all reality, is attempted by the artist. Human beings are placed in the widest possible context, definitely present but often quite small, set as they are within the entire field of the artist's cosmic view.

The contrast between the vision of some artists of my own culture and time, and that of more ancient Oriental artists was striking. Dirty corner versus whole reality. What we call realism today may well betray our preoccupation with detail as we miss the context of our lives, the bigger picture. Do we really see so little, only a bit of ourselves and a slice of existence, isolated from everything else around us? The whole envelope of reality these days seems to escape our attention, perhaps even our interest. The notion of our being set within a broader context appears increasingly difficult for us to grasp. It just may be that many of our spiritual, emotional, ecological, political, and psychological dilemmas are aggravated by our loss of perspective, our being largely microscopic instead of telescopic, tunnel-visioned instead of panorama-visioned.

I recall a point in my college years when I had become quite depressed. There were the usual academic pressures. In addition, I was wrestling with what decision to make regarding the military draft, for these were the years of the Vietnam War. I was to be married in a few months, and the transition from being single and not really knowing myself yet to beginning a life with another human being raised considerable anxiety. With all of these currents swirling in and around me, I finally "caved in."

The college chaplain came to see me, sitting and listening, letting me talk it out. When he rose to leave, satisfied that I was going to survive, I walked outside my apartment with him. It was just sunset on an early fall evening. We stood a moment in the rose light of the setting sun, silent. Then he said, in the most matter-of-fact yet poignant way, "David, after all, there are still beautiful sunsets." He smiled, and left. My problems were still there—my "dirty corner"—but now they seemed surmountable and, in the whole picture of things, not so devastating.

The psalmist looks at everything—"whole reality"—and wonders that God cares for human beings, keeps us "in mind." This is not a shaking of the head in disbelief—how could God care for such wretches! Here is genuine wonder at suddenly seeing human life in its true context, within the fabric of all existence, all creation. In such moments of revelation, there is peace, wonder, thanksgiving, and joy, all at the same time. We are not so big, after all. But we are not so small, either.

Look, It's God!

So we are ambassadors for Christ, since God is
making his appeal through us….
                                        2 Corinthians 5:20a

One day as I pulled up to a gas station, one of the families in our congregation was already at the pumps. While I filled up, the mother got out of her car and came around to me, suppressing a smile. She wanted to tell me what her youngest daughter had said as I drove up: "Look, it's God!" Her mother and I joked about my being God, I feigning puffed-up pride and the like. It was one of those delightful moments when children speak unabashedly out of their creatively confused view of religion.

Of course, the incident made my day and gave me something quite wonderful to think about. I have learned not to toss off children's pronouncements without careful consideration. At one level, certainly I could see how the youngster had come up with her conclusion. Whenever she is at church, I am the one always talking about God. In her juvenile mind, it made sense that I was, for her, God.

There may be more to it than that, however. My mind immediately turned to a favorite passage of scripture, 2 Corinthians 5:16–21. I thought particularly of this verse: "So we are ambassadors for Christ, since God is making his appeal through us." We are Christ's, thus God's, representatives.

In ancient times, the ambassador or courier of a monarch *was*, for all practical purposes, the presence of the one represented. To deal with the representative was to deal with the one represented. In diplomatic affairs, the minister plenipotentiary has a full range of power and authority to deal with a particular matter in the place of the represented government or head of state. We, then, as persons and communities of faith, fully represent God. This is a function both of God's grace, which makes us God's people, and of our openness, our faithfulness to God's purposes and Spirit.

To be a faithful person is to live a life transparent to God, so that, as Paul wrote, God appeals to the world through us. We become channels of what God wants to accomplish, of God's redemptive activity in and for the world. For the person of faith, there exists an intimate relationship between oneself and God. The Gospel of John especially talks about this mutual dwelling, or inter-dwelling, between us and God. Jesus' prayer that his disciples all be one (John 17) is not a hope for the future, at least not that alone. The oneness Jesus prays for is a oneness already given to the disciples through their faith relationship to Jesus. They *are* one with Jesus, just as Jesus is one with God. The sense of the prayer is this: "That they may remain and always be one even as we [Jesus and God] are one."

In the First Letter of John, this unity stands as a matter of love. "God is love, and those who abide in love abide in God, and God abides in them" (4:16b). This inter-dwelling of God and us becomes manifest to others. This is evident in Jesus' belief that in the unity of his followers with one another, with God, and with Jesus himself, the world will encounter God's glorious reality (John 17:21). Is it any surprise, then, that others, including children, might come to know God through those who have given themselves to the life of faith and love? This is only a fulfillment of Jesus' prayer. These are moments when the image of God becomes manifest in us with clarity.

All of this should not make us anxious, however. For it is a matter of God's grace, not our accomplishment or any special quality in us. Certainly, we are not God. There still remains the distinction between Creator and creature. We are keenly aware of the reality of our limitations, our finiteness. Though we live in a world that bespeaks human control and our supposed capacity to accomplish anything we set our minds and ingenuity to, our experiences afford enough evidence that we, in fact, are not ultimately in charge. Nonetheless, my young friend's accolade was not so far off the mark. Perhaps she was simply, in her childlike manner, affirming the gracious relationship we have with God.

When I talk with people about how they have experienced or come to know God in their lives, they uniformly respond, "Through other people." Scriptures, certainly. The church, also, its life and worship. But in a profound and direct way, we encounter and are encountered by God through the lives of persons who reflect God's mercy, compassion, truth, judgment, and grace. God does, indeed, appeal to us through those human ambassadors who live by their faith, through struggles and doubts, as well as joys and triumphs.

"Look, it's God!" What if we lived with these words on the tips of our tongues? What if we looked at others, and ourselves, in this way? Would it not make a difference in the vitality of our living, not to mention the way we treat others who are also God's representatives, those through whom God reaches out to us?

On the other hand, there lies a decisive question in all of this. If we are those through whom God appeals to the world, how are we to live in accordance with that profound knowledge? This poses a challenge to the church, the self-conscious community of God's ambassadors. No, the church is not an elite club of perfect people. The church cannot relapse into a righteousness of works, forgetting that we live by God's grace alone. And yet, persons are drawn toward or repelled from the church by what they do or do not see and experience there. People cannot demand that the church be other than human, without the quirks, tendencies to hurt, and faults that are inherent in all human beings. However, do others not have a certain right to expect the church to *be* the church, that is, to be the vessel, the instrument of God's redemptive love in the world? "Let your light shine before others, so that they may see your good works and give glory to your Father in heaven" (Matthew 5:16).

So, a child's innocent proclamation speaks both of God's grace and God's call. In a particular and important way, we *are* God. We are God's ambassadors, those through whom God graciously chooses to reach out to a broken world. This is fundamentally a matter of God's grace. Yet, we are called to *be* such channels, such ambassadors, so that in our lives others might see and be drawn to God, giving glory to God, and discovering that they, too, are and can be God in this way.

God's Gift to the World

To the church of God that is in Corinth, to
those who are sanctified in Christ Jesus, called
to be saints, together with all those who in
every place call on the name of our Lord Jesus
Christ, both their Lord and ours....

1 Corinthians 1:2

There were kids in school we used to call "stuck up." They
were the sort who aroused your adolescent insecurities so effec-
tively, making you feel inferior because you were from the wrong
part of town, wore the wrong style of clothes, and all that. Being a kid, your skin was sensitive anyway, so you'd respond,
"They really think they're God's gift to the world!"

As years have gone on, I begin to realize that truly conceited
people are few and far between, and that adolescents most often
express their insecurities by overcompensation. Actually, this
doesn't end with adolescence! Most people, I am increasingly
convinced, grow up with a lack of self-worth in varying degrees.
Our outwardly brazen strutting usually hides a weak self-image.
With a society that is so success-crazed and competition-ori-
ented, the very structures and values around us work against
those who do not feel good about themselves to begin with and
erode self-worth in those who may have a basically strong ego.

Over the years, a different and revolutionary thought has
crept into my head: We *are*, each of us, God's gift to the world!
Yes, we can say it aloud and believe it in our hearts. This is the
message of biblical faith. As people who have responded to God's
love and seek to live our lives along that path, we are, indeed,
important and have much to offer. "You are the light of the

world," said Jesus in the Sermon on the Mount. There need be no false humility here, for no vain pride is promoted. Paul, without batting an eye, addressed those to whom he wrote his letters as "saints," *hagioi*, holy ones. How poignant that he even spoke in this way to the cantankerous Christians at Corinth! Well, actually, the salutation of his first Corinthian letter reminded them that they were "called to be" saints. Reading through the letter, we find that the problem lay in their forgetting that they *were* saints. However, in the opening words of the second Corinthian letter, we find Paul straightforwardly calling this same group "saints."

We have labored under the burdensome and problematic doctrine of "original sin" for so long that we have forgotten about "original righteousness" or "original goodness" (Genesis 1). We have forgotten the image of God in which we were created, male and female. To hear God's call in Christ, to respond with a life centered in him is to be a "new creation"(2 Corinthians 5), God's gift to the world, one through whom God works to bring new life.

The church itself is not just any get-together, but a "communion of saints," those who strive to see themselves and others as gifts of God to the world, calling forth that giftedness in one another, without jealousy or fear. "To each is given the manifestation of the Spirit for the common good" (1 Corinthians 12:7). What a transformation occurs when we stop functioning under a false sense of humility that keeps our giftedness stifled and unshared, and begin exercising that giftedness, especially the simple gift of ourselves, for the good of all! What a difference occurs when we begin to see each other through the eyes of God, perceiving that we each are, indeed, God's gift to the world!

> ...for God did not give us a spirit of cowardice, but rather a spirit of power and of love and of self-discipline.
>
> 2 Timothy 1:7

Voice from the Whirlwind

A minster's day off can be a strange thing. One February day, I awoke feeling groggy from the previous day of long hours filled with several emotionally taxing events. I had planned to spend the day hiking in the mountains. My mind and body, however, suffered a numbness and inertia that made staying in bed far more attractive!

I have learned that in such states I need to force myself out, away from town, people, and familiar surroundings, getting physically distant from the web of work and worries. So I dragged myself out to my car and headed to the Peaks of Otter, only a thirty-minute drive from Lynchburg.

As the miles rolled by under the tires, my state improved steadily. I was grateful that I had forced myself out onto the road. By the time I pulled into the parking lot at the foot of Sharp Top, my body and spirit felt a tremble of anticipation of the trail ahead.

The Peaks of Otter are two mountains in the Blue Ridge chain, standing side by side, each about four thousand feet at the summit. These mountains have had a strong allure for people for centuries. Native American hunting parties are said to have felt from the Peaks a powerful spiritual attraction. I can believe that, for, growing up close by, I have spent many hours and days here. In the throes of adolescence, I had found solace and an important expanding of my spirit walking the trails of Sharp Top and its sibling, Flat Top (pedestrian names for such grand mountains!).

I've hiked the Sharp Top trail for over thirty years. It is familiar to my feet and mind. And yet, there is such a diversity of terrain that I am never bored. Switching back and forth up the mountainside, the trail introduces the hiker to expansive as well as subtle views, each varied further by the time of day or season of the year. For a mile and a half, one moves through groves of mountain laurel or alongside huge boulders. The trail winds steadily up, a challenge but not so strenuous as to prevent contemplation.

That day the sky had a kaleidoscope quality. Winter in Virginia consists of frequently vacillating temperatures. This day saw a springlike warmth losing its grip before the assault of an incoming cold front. Snow had been predicted by nightfall, but I was skeptical.

Arriving at the top, which actually has two summits, I chose the lesser one, called Buzzard's Roost. The last several hundred yards to the pile of boulders that cap the mountain are the most strenuous, because one's legs are tired and ready to quit. At least mine were that day, and I wasn't in a greatly self-challenging mood.

The rocks at Buzzard's Roost form an outcrop on the western side. Atop them, I was in the full force of the wind, which by then had a cold bite. I backed down a few feet, nestling into a crevice. Stretching out to the south and southwest was the expanse of Bedford County. A patchwork of farms, their meadows and fields in hues of blue, brown, and dull green, caught the sunlight sweeping down between the shuttling clouds. In the distance, about twenty-five miles, I guessed, was a sliver of gold, luminous with a satiny quality. This was Smith Mountain Lake. The sunlight glanced off the fingers of the lake so that it appeared like a bright wound in the earth.

I brought out my peanut butter crackers and thermos of coffee, contentedly eating and drinking in the shelter of the rocks.

After about an hour, I stood up to prepare for the walk down. When I turned around, I found the weather sneaking in behind me from the north—a dense bank of clouds rolling in on the mountainside, peppering everything with freezing rain. My immediate response was dread. The return trip would find me wet, cold, and uncomfortable. Suddenly, however, my mood shifted like the clouds of that sky. So what if I got rained on? The thirty-minute walk down the side of Sharp Top, receiving the pummeling of the weather, now offered an odd sort of excitement.

Off I strode, zipping up my flannel vest and yanking out my stocking cap and gloves. Mindless of the sleetlike rain…no, not mindless of it, but enfolded by and immersed in it…I examined this feeling of delight at being so exposed on the side of the mountain. How protected my life seems to be! I become so accustomed to schedules and calendars, predicted and predictable events, that I stand in danger of thinking my life is not vulnerable, that everything runs like clockwork. How deadening! What an illusion! How refreshing it had been to stand atop that mountain, realizing that it and the view around me would long outlast my eye-blink of a life! I thought how feverish and hellish we make our lives by overestimating the importance of our projects, meetings, schemes, noble efforts, and the like. Perhaps it all matters. Of course it all matters. But ultimately the world greets our self-importance with silence and the currents of ages that flow far beyond our little horizons in both directions. How good it was to be vulnerable, exposed to the winds and the gracious indifference of the icy rain!

Then the LORD answered Job out of the whirlwind:…
"Gird up your loins like a man,
   I will question you,
      and you shall declare to me.
"Where were you when I laid the foundation of the
   earth?
   Tell me, if you have understanding."

Job 38:1, 3–4

Reconsidering Eros

O taste and see that the LORD is good....

Psalm 34:8

I know that there is nothing better for them than to
be happy and enjoy themselves as long as they live;
moreover, it is God's gift that all should eat and
drink and take pleasure in all their toil.

Ecclesiastes 3:12–13

Springtime arrives, and I can't help but fall in love with life
again, by upbringing, temperament, or whatever reason. This,
for me, is *eros*, that much-maligned sort of love that embraces,
delights in, and desires the pleasure and beauty of life. *Eros* is
that love that savors a strain of music, a line of poetry, evenings
in a favorite café with my wife, fishing on a quiet lake, walking
on a beach at sunset, or—dare I say it!—the pleasures of our
sexuality. A part of me is devoted to *eros*. I cannot be, nor do I
wish to be, cured of it.

Somewhere along the way, *eros* was demoted in favor of *agape*,
the self-giving, sacrificial, "spiritual" sort of love. Perhaps this
was as it should have been. I believe, however, that this dimin-
ishing of *eros* was more the work of particular moral traditions
rather than something inherent in Scripture itself. *Agape* became, in the practice of stringent piety, a bloodless, joyless af-
fair. And yet, I think that *eros*, passion for life, for the world,
underlies the "greater love" that is taught in Hebrew and Christian Scriptures, or at least is to be its companion.

The book of Ecclesiastes records the experiment of the
"preacher" in finding out what good there is in life. He sees

much "vanity," emptiness, about him. Yet, in the end, he comes to a less lofty, more creaturely appreciation of the life God has given to human beings. Being happy and enjoying oneself, having a definite taste for life, is, in the writer's conclusion, a "holy" business. The words of Psalm 34, "O taste and see that the LORD is good," certainly lend themselves to a typically psalmic appreciation of the world God has created for us to experience and enjoy. Another rendering of the verse resonates with the investigations of the writer of Ecclesiastes: "Find out for yourself how good the LORD is" (TEV).

Jesus himself was maligned as a glutton and drunkard because he didn't conform to the piety of "religious" sorts (Matthew 11:18–19). To sour-faced strict pietists Jesus announced the feasting that was more appropriate than their fasting. He likened the in-breaking of the kingdom of God to a wedding, a party (Mark 2:18–22). I doubt that Jesus could not tell such splendid parables, incorporating so many elements of the natural world, without an underlying passion for the world itself as God's creation.

Certainly a life of unmitigated *eros* can become destructively self-indulgent and spiritually deadening. But *agape* without *eros* runs the risk of a "spiritualized" life detached from one's God-created humanity and the creation, if not also the Creator. *Eros*, love that desires, that is "full of" life, and *agape*, love that gives, that shares, cannot cancel each other out without distorting life as a whole.

If all this strikes you as a tad irreligious, go back and read a few lines of the psalms that rejoice in the creation. For that matter, reread the Genesis accounts of creation, wherein God pronounces everything made *good*. Turn to the pages of the Song of Solomon, taking in a few lines of sensuous Hebrew love poetry. Then, by all means, go out and take a walk on a fine spring evening…and enjoy!

A Biblical Valentine

Let him kiss me with the kisses of his mouth!
For your love is better than wine....
                                    Song of Solomon 1:2

These are words suited to a Valentine's Day card, are they
not? They are also words fitting for the church, though we seldom, if ever, hear them read on a Sunday morning. They are
the opening words of a book of lyric love poems found in the
canon of Scripture—the Song of Solomon, or Song of Songs.

What are such sensuous verses doing in a nice book like the
Bible? Their place in the canon was not a "natural" fit, it seems,
and the Song of Solomon had some difficulty making it as "scripture." However, the wisdom of those who finally set the canon
prevailed, though not without a struggle, and this celebration
of human love was included in the writings of the community
of faith.

This collection of poems explores and celebrates erotic, pas-
sionate love. Sexuality is placed squarely in the context of
creational, that is, God-given, reality. In explicit as well as subtle
ways, the Song of Solomon exults in the joys and longings of
human love. The maiden dreams of searching for her lover:

Upon my bed at night
    I sought him whom my soul loves;
I sought him, but found him not;
    I called him, but he gave no answer. (3:1)

In simile and metaphor, the lovers describe each other
through eyes of longing affection:

How beautiful you are, my love,
    how very beautiful!
Your eyes are doves
    behind your veil.
Your hair is like a flock of goats,
    moving down the slopes of Giliad....
Your lips are like a crimson thread,
    and your mouth is lovely. (4:1,3)

In these poems sensual love is not denigrated by comparison to some loftier, more "spiritual" love. The sacred depth of just this kind of love is expressed:

Set me as a seal upon your heart,
    as a seal upon your arm;
for love is strong as death,
    passion fierce as the grave....
Many waters cannot quench love,
    neither can floods drown it.
If one offered for love
    all the wealth of his house,
    it would be utterly scorned. (8:6a, 7)

The Song of Solomon defies all attempts to "spiritualize" its sentiments. It is not an allegory of the love of God for God's people. Neither is it an allegory of the love between Christ and the church or the individual believer. Such attempts at allegorization have been made throughout the centuries, but stand on very shaky ground. An affirmation of sensual love, the Song of Solomon is a bouquet of poetry gathered by a community that was not embarrassed by its humanity, but saw it as part of God's good creation. "God saw everything that he had made, and, indeed, it was very good" (Genesis 1:31).

My hunch is that we need to hear from the Song of Solomon more often these days. How ambivalent we are about our sexuality! We drift between two extremes. On the one hand, sexuality arouses guilt and repression. The "covering of our nakedness" that is part of the Genesis 3 story was not meant by early Israel to express a God-intended shame. Rather, here was a narrative of regrettable loss of created innocence, of being naked and unashamed. The church bears much responsibility for this avoidance and repression of our sexuality. You simply don't talk about things like that in church! The other extreme, related to the first as a kind of reverse image, is violence and self-gratification in the ways we treat others sexually. If what is natural and good becomes a matter of shame and guilt, repression eventually, if not inevitably, erupts in sickness.

The Song of Solomon finds its place among other "wisdom" books in Hebrew Scriptures. Together, these writings point the community of faith toward thoughtfulness and discerning in matters of human living. All aspects of our humanity come under God's lordship and goodness, including sensual love, and need to be examined in that light. When set in this context, human sexuality and sensuality stand a greater chance of being healthy and a source of joy.

True, issues of human sexuality are complex. The Song of Solomon does not pretend to be a textbook on sexual morality. Yet the presence of this book in our Bible can correct us at the starting-point of our thinking about sexuality. Perhaps by recognizing the important contribution of this book to the church's literature and faith-perspective, we can help one another, young people and adults alike, affirm the beautiful, enjoyable, and significant place of sexuality in our lives. This would indeed be a healthy beginning.

And so, from the Song of Solomon, happy Valentine's Day!

Lent

Easter

Delivered from Anxiousness

"Do not worry about tomorrow...."
Matthew 6:34a

When our children were small, I developed, quite by accident, a lifesaving habit. I would arrive home from work, tired and preoccupied, also dragging the weight of a father's guilt for having to be away from wife and family so much. So, off I would go for a walk down the street with my children in the late afternoon. I pulled one in a wagon, the other scratching along the pavement on a tricycle.

At first, as we walked, my gait was still hurried from the pace of the day's work. Impatience flared up inside me as my children dawdled here and there, inspecting this piece of gravel or that discarded candy wrapper. I wanted to "get on with it." Their world was so small and minute and unhurried, mine so frenetic and full of "responsibility." In their world, time was a playground, in mine, a tyrant—not a second to "waste"!

However, I discovered on these late afternoon forays that, little by little, as I followed my children along their meandering way, my inner sense of hurriedness and anxiousness melted away. At first, I felt that I was driving them along, like sluggish cattle. Later, I realized that they were leading me, luring me into their world. As I became more content to let them take the lead, I felt myself being renewed and refreshed, the world coming back into perspective, the way one feels after recovering from a fever. I began to discern how much of my adult world was an exaggeration, even an illusion about what truly matters. After a while, I found that I was looking forward to getting home in time for these walks of ours and felt out of sorts when I missed them.

Not long after this discovery, we moved to another state where I undertook a new pastorate. My wife and I went ahead to meet the moving van, and the children stayed with grandparents. By the time our children arrived at the new home, I felt myself strung between two powerful feelings—homesickness for the familiarity left behind, and anxiety over what lay ahead, a new job with exciting but unknown prospects. We have such moments, when we feel ourselves stretched out on the rack of time between an irretrievable past and a future veiled in utter openness.

The children arrived. Our daughter, then two years old, headed straight for her new bedroom. I followed to see what she would make of it. Her first task was to give attention, one by one, to her toys. She sat on the floor, and I sat with her. She played, absorbed, in her own way making this "home." I watched. We talked about this and that. Soon I realized that past and future had evaporated. She had led me back to the land of the present, and to the realization that, rooted in the present, one finds strength and peace to face the future.

"So do not worry about tomorrow…." Young children seem to feel naturally at home in the present. They can be our teachers, our leaders, who point the way out of disabling and useless preoccupations. We fritter away our energies by incessantly mulling over the past and fretting over the future. To receive each moment as a gift, to be alive and alert in the present—this is true freedom and joy. It is the kingdom of God. And unless we can receive it as a child does, we cannot enter it (Mark 10:15).

The Nervous Soul/
The Quieted Soul

O LORD, my heart is not lifted up,
    my eyes are not raised too high;
I do not occupy myself with things
    too great and too marvelous for me.
But I have calmed and quieted my soul,
    like a child quieted at its mother's breast;
    like a child that is quieted is my soul.
O Israel, hope in the LORD
    from this time forth and for evermore.
Psalm 131 (RSV)

This brief psalm speaks of the "quieted soul." The world we live in creates in us "nervous souls." Our schedules are over-packed. We live on the edge, ever-vigilant for the next deadline, appointment, or demand upon us. Many of us have similar nightmares—we dream that we are late for a crucial appointment, or that we show up unprepared for a big test or meeting. Our souls are made nervous, too, by information. How important it is that we have much information about what is going on in the world! Christians should know as much as possible about this world that "God so loved." Sometimes, however, we become too full of news, too full of information, and since much of it distresses us, our souls become nervous. We fret over things but feel powerless. And often our worrying keeps us from doing what we can because we feel frozen in fear, anxiousness, or a sense of dread. All of this winds us tight on the inside, for we want to be in control and have nothing take us by surprise. Yet we feel more like victims, passive and defensive.

The nervous soul is a crowded soul, always on guard. The psalm speaks of the quieted soul that has room for God and a capacity to "rest in God." This psalm speaks of times when our hearts are not "lifted up"—moments of discouragement, being overwhelmed, or simply numb (nervous feelings). The eyes can no longer keep their tense vigilance (nervous looking) and are lowered. The mind becomes overloaded and must let go of pre-occupations (nervous thinking). The psalmist has calmed and quieted the soul. That is a good definition of prayer—the calming and quieting of our souls, of our selves in God's presence. We find that we can rest in God's presence, just as a child, once upset, nestles securely in its parent's arms.

The quieted soul can let go of its anxious hold on life in order to be embraced by God, receiving life as a gift. Then life becomes renewable and room is made for hope—"O Israel, hope in the LORD." The quieted soul is ready to listen to God, to be reclaimed from the "nervousness" of the world. Then, having been calmed and reclaimed by God, we can be sent into the world again to live more fruitfully even in the midst of a nervous world.

In returning and rest you shall be saved;
        in quietness and in trust shall be your strength.
                                        Isaiah 30:15

Patience Threshold

"If it seems to tarry, wait for it;
  it will surely come, it will not delay."
                    Habakkuk 2:3

We have purchased our first microwave oven. What an improvement! Now it takes so little time to prepare a meal or make our popcorn. What a truly helpful and wondrous invention for busy families!

And yet…I now find myself at times standing impatiently in front of this technological speed-up device, waiting for something to finish cooking or heating up. I notice that my "patience threshold" has shrunk. My capacity for waiting diminishes with the more speed-up devices I accumulate. This carries over into other areas of my life, and I become decreasingly able to "take time" for things to happen.

There is a spiritual trade-off that comes with hurry-up living. We hurry ourselves. We hurry others—our children, our spouses, our students, our friends. We hurry our careers, often shifting directions before we have begun to gain enough experience to give us a sense of accomplishment or satisfaction. If something doesn't give immediate gratification or results, we are tempted to "change horses."

With more efficiency and speed, we increase our sense of control over everything, as well, making things happen just when and how we want them. Underneath it all, however, our fundamental belief in God's activity in life is eroded. Everything, we think, happens on the human level. In reality, though, our sense of being in control is more illusory than we thought.

How contradictory for me, believing as I do in the importance of "inward" time, the timing of the Spirit, to be so caught up in rapidity and efficiency! In my quest for greater speed, I forfeit the time to see, to notice, to listen, to wait for something important to come about. With a constantly shrinking patience threshold, my attentiveness to God's presence and activity in life becomes dulled.

It is easy to forget that with God things move more slowly. For forty years the people of Israel wandered in the wilderness in order to learn faith, that is, trustful following of God. The prophets of Israel spoke generally in a time when dislocation and intense spiritual questioning "slowed down" the nation. Habakkuk, writing in the years preceding the fall of the Jerusalem temple in 587 B.C.E., had many questions: *How long* shall I cry for help, and God not hear? (1:2). Why does God make me see wrongs and look upon trouble? (1:3). Why is God silent when the wicked swallow up the righteous? (1:13). These are "slow down" questions; they have no quick answers. They cause deep pondering and searching.

So, the word comes to Habakkuk from God:

Write the vision;
    make it plain on tablets,
    so that a runner may read it.
For there is still a vision for the appointed time;
    it speaks of the end, and does not lie....
It will surely come, it will not delay.
Habakkuk 2:2b–3

The vision of new life *will* come. God does not delay. But God's time is not necessarily suited to our schedules. Get ready to announce the message boldly, but only when you have been given something to say. Wait. Watch. Listen.

Consider Jesus, also. He spent forty days in the desert before his message and ministry were ready to go. The Gospel of Mark tells us that Jesus did not even want the disciples to reveal his identity to anyone (8:29–30). Isn't that self-defeating? Jesus, it would appear, had a problem with "success"! When offered a quick victory and power over the kingdoms of the world, Jesus declined, holding out for a kingdom of another world (Matthew 4:1–11). Finally, instead of a triumphant coup in the city of Jerusalem, he was stopped cold, crucified. All of this in obedience to God's time, God's movement, the timing of God's Spirit working in and through the human Spirit and human history.

It takes great discipline for us to wait, to slow down and be attentive to the lessons of our faith in the midst of a hurry-up world. It is not a quick course! We can practice waiting, however, in even the little things of life so that, bit by bit, we refuse to rush others or ourselves. We learn to relinquish our desire to control everything, growing increasingly sensitive and responsive to the timing and pace of God's Spirit.

> I will stand at my watchpost,
>   and station myself on the rampart;
> I will keep watch to see
>   what God will say to me....
> Habakkuk 2:1

Unless God Builds the House

Unless the Lord *builds* the house,
   those who build it labor in vain.
Unless the LORD guards the city,
   the guard keeps watch in vain.
It is in vain that you rise up early
   and go late to rest,
eating the bread of anxious toil;
   for God gives sleep to his beloved.

Psalm 127:1–2

A common complaint these days is: "I am so busy that I can't keep up with everything! I'm involved in too much. I must give up something. I must learn to say no."

Saying no is an important lesson that many people, including myself, are learning. We probably do favor too many requests, on the false assumption that we possess unlimited resources to deal with every problem or task that comes our way. Also, there is that seditious fear in us that if we say no, people won't like us! It is a good thing to learn to say no.

Part of the dilemma may be that we attach great value to "being busy." Energy, industry, full schedules, getting things accomplished—these seem to comprise our contemporary badges of self-worth. We may well be suspicious, in fact, of persons who are not busy all the time, who have "time on their hands." Idleness is the devil's playground, and all that. We feel guilty if we ourselves are not "on the go," constantly reaping accomplishments.

All of this may account, in part, for what seems to be an epidemic of "burnout." Being incessantly in motion, on the go, keeping multitudes of commitments that we try to balance like jugglers eventually results in extreme stress. Our internal reserves run dry in the face of external demands and internal compulsions. The result? Exhaustion—physical, mental, and spiritual. Also, there grows in us like a dark, heavy cloud, the guilt which says, "I'm doing so many things but I don't feel like I'm doing any of them very well." I suspect a good many of us suffer from this vicious syndrome.

What of the spiritual dimension of overcommitment and excessive stress? When it comes to our faith, we are certainly called to "do" things. Christian faith is essentially a *life*, the life of loving action in the world after the pattern of Jesus Christ. Jesus calls us to follow him in a ministry of compassion and mercy, justice and peace, of caring for others and the creation. *Doing* is very important. But I do not find anything about Jesus that leads me to believe he wants us to be dragging around as though the whole weight of the world rests on our shoulders, dogged by guilty feelings, resentment, and, in the end, leading a joyless, compulsive life.

"We love because God first loved us," says the First Letter of John. Our doing is a response to love, God's fundamental and prior action in and for the world. Biblical faith talks first about what God has done, is doing, and will do. God does the building, the watching. Of course we need human builders and watchers. However, all our efforts end up in anxiousness without trust in God's prior and ultimate sovereignty over and care of us and the world. Human activity is good, even essential, but is not everything, and risks being frenetic activism unless rooted in God's action.

"God has no hands but our hands." I have heard this little aphorism all my life. Now, however, I think we need to call into question the one-dimensional emphasis on the human side, or at least develop a wider context in which to understand the significance of our actions. The psalmist reminds us that God stands as the primary actor in the renewal and redemption of life, not human beings. We are called to be part of what God is already doing, indeed, has already done, in and for the world. If we become beguiled into thinking that everything rests on our efforts, we eventually fall into despair, cynicism, or zealous and misguided, even violent, activism.

As people of faith, we need to cultivate something of a spiritual gyroscope that keeps in us a balance between proper human responsibility and consciousness of God's dominion over life, including our own lives. Here we do well to think of a rhythmic movement between action and prayer, work and rest, speaking and silence.

In the psalm, what does God do but give us sleep? One side effect of stress and anxiety is hypervigilance—sleeplessness. We cannot go to sleep because we think that life cannot go on unless we perpetually stand our guard, unless we solve every problem, tie up every loose end. Hard as it may be for us responsibly minded individuals to grasp, life does and indeed will go on without us. Certainly, we have an effect and need to live with purpose. Our lives do make a difference beyond their seemingly small circles. However, we become spiritually empty when we believe we must be perpetually "on the job." The beloved Psalm 23 could well be translated this way: "God leads me beside waters of rest; God renews life within me." For faith to be faith, there needs to be a passive, receptive side to our living, so that we can fully receive the renewal God gives us.

Jesus seemed quite concerned that people not live anxious, heavily burdened lives. "Therefore I tell you, do not worry about your life, what you will eat or what you will drink…"(Matthew 6:25). "Do not let your hearts be troubled. Believe in God, believe also in me" (John 14:1). In other words, trust in me, trust in God. Jesus apparently knew our penchant for hyperactivity, super-responsibility, and hypervigilance. Without taking away his call to active discipleship, to lay down our lives for his sake and for the gospel, Jesus witnesses to a faith that counsels us to rest, to be at peace, to be still and know that God is God (Psalm 46:10).

The life of faith knows the profound connection between rest and motion, between passivity and activity, prayer and obedient service in the world. Our lives begin and end in the rest that God gives. Only out of such rest can a truly trustful and effective life of faith be attained.

When the Time Is Right

May the God of steadfastness and encouragement grant you to live in harmony with one another, in accordance with Christ Jesus, so that together you may with one voice glorify the God and Father of our Lord Jesus Christ.

Romans 15:5–6

[Love] does not insist on its own way....

1 Corinthians 13:5

I like these words from Paul's Letter to the Romans very much. They tell me about the nature of God's love toward us. Is God's love coercive or dictatorial? No. Does God manipulate us or otherwise take away our freedom to choose what is right or good? No. God's love is known for its steadfastness—from the Greek *hupomonos*, meaning patience, forbearance, perseverance. God's love is also encouraging—from *parakleseos*, meaning exhortation, comfort, consolation. God's love exudes a kind of pressure upon our lives that urges us, calls us forward into itself. It is, however, more like the "pressure" of the sun upon the earth than that of a forced march.

One summer our daughter finally learned to ride a bicycle. Few experiences offer such gratification as that miraculous moment when a child suddenly takes off on two wheels! The change is epochal—one moment flip-flopping from foot to foot, the next breezing down the driveway under one's own steam, balanced, confident, filled with exhilaration. What happens in that moment when one finds one's balance is, for me, though explainable at one level, an utter mystery and miracle.

How I had wanted my daughter to learn to ride a bike, afraid she would remain too timid to exert the effort, to take the risk! How I had wished for her the experience of the distinctive rush of self-confidence and freedom that comes in the moment of mastery of that skill! How I had pushed at times, to no avail! Then I realized anew that each person must do things, must come to such moments, in his or her own way and time. We can instruct, urge, explain, lecture, rant, or otherwise push, but little of that achieves the goal. Encouragement, yes; coercion, no. In the end, our daughter had to experience the *kairos*, that New Testament word for the "right time," within the stream of her own efforts and will. That is the way it must be for each of us when it comes to growing as people of faith.

Paul's insight into the nature of God's love can help us understand this: In matters of becoming truly human, as God has made and intends us to be, we are not coerced by God. God does not drive us forward, but encouragingly, sometimes confrontationally, calls and then steadfastly waits for us.

If God so loves us, is this not how we are to love one another? (1 John 4). May this not be the harmony in which we are to live with one another? Growth in love, as we know it in Jesus Christ, does not happen for everyone at the same time, in the same way. And we cannot presume to make it so for each other. We are, of course, to be concerned with one another's lives of faith. Yet we cannot presume to know what is good for others or put them on our timetables. Nor can we rush into another's life with a pretentious and controlling spirit that is only thinly masked by our conviction that we are, after all, acting lovingly.

We may, however, stand by one another, patiently, encouragingly, steadfastly, ready to give support, comfort, and finally a shout of joy when the *kairos* comes, when others at last "take off." We do not belong to one another in such a way that we may dare decide anything for the other. The harmony that Paul wished for the Roman church, and for the whole church, would finally be a gift from God's hand, a gift they would receive and live out of in their own good time, and in God's.

And so, I remain deeply grateful for our daughter's accomplishment, for I have remembered something important about God's love and ours. I realize afresh that my patience is shorter than God's, my wisdom shallower, my vision more shortsighted, and that my love always stands in need of being informed by God's love.

Pigging-out in the Wilderness

"You shall eat not only one day, or two days…
but for a whole month—until it comes out of
your nostrils and becomes loathsome to you—
because you have rejected the LORD who is among
you…."

Numbers 11:19a, 20a

Some years ago a term emerged among young people—"pigging-out." This meant eating to an absurd extreme, as in, "Let's go to McDonald's and pig-out!" Such a thing could only be possible in a culture such as ours. We are able to pig-out on nearly anything—entertainment, clothes, endless fads and whims, even relationships.

In the book of Numbers we find a strange tale from the wilderness wanderings of Israel. A group of rabble-rousers (11:4) takes up the complaint heard nearly from the beginning of the Exodus—"Oh that we had stayed in Egypt! At least we had enough to eat and relative leisure, not this aimless wandering about, eating tasteless manna!" God had responded to the people's hunger in the first place by providing the sticky, flaky manna. But the people grew tired of that, too, and craved a more exotic cuisine. The oppression from which they had been liberated was fading from their memories. Now immediate matters of comfort and diet had overtaken larger issues of theology or spirituality!

Moses takes the people's complaint to God. His feelings are clear (verses 10–15). He is bone-weary from carrying these shortsighted people around. Essentially Moses says to God, "If you care at all for me, you'll kill me and put me out of my misery!"

God's response is innovative. Through Moses, God tells the people, "You want meat? I'll give you meat! Not just for one or two days, but for a whole month. And you'll eat so much of it that it will come out of your nostrils! You'll be sick of it!" Not a pretty image! The people will be allowed to "pig-out." They are given the freedom and resources to follow their appetites to the extreme. The story ends on a grim note. God provides plenty of quail. The people gather and cook the birds. But just as they are sinking their teeth in, God sends a plague that kills off the original rabble-rousers. They are buried at a place dubbed *Kibroth-hattaavah*, "graves of craving."

Our consumer culture trains us to acquire whatever promises to fulfill our wants or needs. Advertising becomes the skilled manipulation of appetites for endless supplies of goods and services. Newer and newer products emerge for needs we never knew we had. Interesting niceties, but hardly essential to life. A consumerist mentality works its way into our thoughts and actions so that we come to believe that to live is to consume and to consume is to live.

The consumerist philosophy creates its counterpart in the religious sphere—a consumerist spirituality. Israel's craving bespoke a crisis of faith. Faith has to do with openness, risk, change, trustful reliance upon God. Consumerism proclaims that life becomes meaningful only in the security one feels with acquired possessions and immediate gratification. When consumerism enters the church, the church is viewed as a consumer item. There are, for instance, complaints about worship—the sermon too long, the choir off-key, the hymns unfamiliar, the children too noisy! The consumer attitude creates an entertainment expectation, so that worship is expected to inspire, stimulate, move, or make us feel this or that. When the church fails to "deliver," we become dissatisfied and withdraw, going "shopping" for a church that suits us.

We might do well to look again at the age-old practice of fasting. At its best, fasting has served as a self-discipline that enables a clearer focusing on one's relationship to God and one's fellow human beings. Fasting is the practice of "doing without" in order to clarify God's will in one's life and to find a more faithful expression of that will. Consumerism is the practice of "not doing without," of accumulating. The two movements, one toward faith and the other toward self-centered security, come into spiritual conflict. The more "full" our lives become in terms of gratification and material things, the less room there is in our lives for God and others.

I notice what happens in my own life with the acquisition of more things. An automatic dishwasher. A television and video cassette player. A self-propelled lawnmower. Then things break. Money paid out for upkeep and operation. Time spent delivering appliances to the shop. The managing of things becomes complex and time-consuming. My life becomes increasingly preoccupied with overseeing all this "stuff" and less given to matters more beneficial to my own spirit and to the world.

What is the ethic of the Christian gospel? Whoever would follow Christ must *deny* the self and pick up a cross and follow Jesus. Whoever tries to save (hoard) his or her life will lose it;

and whoever loses life for Christ's sake and the good news will find it (Mark 8:34–38). Here is the paradox of our faith—in giving up, we receive; in losing, we find; in forgetting the self, we find true selfhood. The kind of fasting we undertake in the face of self-centered consumerism can be a key to recovering the gospel and our very lives, if not also the life of the creation that is so ravaged by our pigging-out lifestyles.

When we refrain from pigging-out, we remain faithful to the long-range journey of God's redemptive work in the world. In the face of the pigging-out character of our culture, we remain faithful to the pouring-out of God's love.

Let the same mind be in you that was in
Christ Jesus,
>who, though he was in the form of God,
>>did not regard equality with God
>>as something to be exploited,
>but emptied himself....

Philippians 2:5–7a

Letting Our Children Go

"There was a man who had two sons. The younger
of them said to his father, 'Father, give me the share
of the property that will belong to me.' So he
divided his property between them."

Luke 15:11–13

Our children now are teenagers. How could anyone have
prepared us for this! I wouldn't have understood had they tried.
I don't mean simply the erratic behavior of early adolescents. It
is not what *they* are going through that has struck me full force,
but what I am going through as I try to catch up to a new
parenting role.

I am anxious about our children, what they will do, what
they will become, what they will achieve, what they will suffer.
Beneath my anxiousness lies the feeling of losing control. How
we delude ourselves with this sense of being in control! Mental
pictures of how the world is and how people are fix themselves
in us, and we begin to live out of those pictures, not the reality
of the world or of people. But then the actuality hits us. The
world is not as we pictured it. People will simply not conform
to the ways we construe them. This holds true for our children,
as well. I think that the entry of our children into adolescence at
the same time as we enter midlife gives us a double dose of
reality. Our illusions quickly fade. This is a time of reckoning!

Did I ever have this control over our children that I now
feel I am losing? Certainly, when they were smaller, I could "push
them around," set boundaries, even make decisions affecting
them without consulting them. Now they are increasingly out
in the world on their own, making their own relationships and

decisions, over which I have a decreasing amount of direct influence. Our relationship must include more dialogue and compromise than before. Perhaps my children are moving in directions that concern me, that are different from what I envisioned for them. Perhaps they will not "turn out" quite the way I wanted. It is all very confusing, and fearful!

What I experience is the excruciating process of inwardly letting go. Children do not, in fact, *belong* to us. We forget, or never recognize, that they are singular creatures, with an autonomy that is never fully under our control. Influence, yes. Control, no. Come adolescence, if we continue to try "pushing them around," there can be an intense backlash. They are asserting the inward mystery of their own being, which is to them a mystery, as well. For parents, this is a time of extreme caution, discerning when and where boundaries must be set, when and where they must be removed.

On a recent Sunday, the Gospel lesson was the story of the "prodigal son," misnamed, for it is so much more about the patient, welcoming love the of father. The story is also about the other son who thought he had to earn his father's love by hard work and being responsible. What a dynamic story this is! Full of power and meaning, never exhausted, never "finished" in our understanding of it! Hearing the story this time around, I was impressed with the "letting go" nature of the father's love. When the younger son asked for the inheritance, the father simply handed it over. He likely knew that his son was embarking on a disastrous adventure, sowing his "wild oats." The father could have been deeply hurt by his son's self-centeredness, for by taking the inheritance before his father's death, the son was, in effect, treating his father as dead. But the father let him go, without scolding, manipulation, or a lecture, without instilling a guilt that would keep the son psychologically tethered to home.

How astounding is this letting-go love! I think that this extraordinarily loving act of letting go gave the son the freedom to "come to himself" and return home. This "coming to ourselves" is something we each must do in our own lifetimes, in our own ways, within the fabric of our own lives and experiences. "Coming to ourselves" might well mean awakening to our own being. "Coming home" may mean finding our own lives in the gracious love of God who rejoices over us.

Perhaps the most challenging task of parenting is learning how to let *our* children go—to themselves, to life, to God.

Parental Surprises

Then the king will say to those at his right hand,
"Come, you that are blessed by my Father,
inherit the kingdom prepared for you from
the foundation of the world; for I was hungry
and you gave me food, I was thirsty and you
gave me something to drink, I was a stranger
and you welcomed me, I was naked and you
gave me clothing, I was sick and you took care
of me, I was in prison and you visited me."
Matthew 25:34–36

Our son traveled to a Baltimore Orioles game at their new stadium, the guest of a friend and his father. When he returned, I was anxious to hear about it, so I fished for details. No luck. A fourteen-year-old can play his cards pretty close to his chest, especially with parents!

A few days later, however, as we rode in the car, my son shared with me, quite out of the blue, a story from his trip. "Steve and I were walking around the Baltimore Harbor," he said. A pause. "There was this homeless man." Another pause.

I didn't know whether or not to probe. I chose to wait. "You know what we did?" No, I said, what did you do? "We each gave him five dollars." I was stunned! Five dollars is no small sum to a teenager, especially one as tight-fisted as our son. His financial sights were consistently trained on expensive basketball shoes or Nintendo games.

One always hopes that instilling values in our children actually works. And yet, given the maelstrom of adolescence, one can never be sure. At a certain point, we simply have to trust that something is taking place at a deeper level than we can perceive.

At my son's revelation, I tendered a very pleased affirmation. I moderated my euphoria somewhat. With teenagers, parents must be careful about too much exuberance over what we see as a parental triumph. It might backfire!

"You know," my son continued, "I don't think too many fourteen-year-olds would give a homeless man five dollars." He said this without a hint of conceit, but with a kind of sober observation as he reflected on this obviously important experience in his life. Then he added: "When we gave him the money, he said, 'God bless you.'" Theology, too! My heart soared. My son had touched holiness, though I dared not suggest that to him. I don't think I needed to do so. I could see it on his face.

Gracious Interruptions

But when Jesus saw this, he was indignant and
said to them, "Let the little children come to
me; do not stop them; for it is to such as these
that the kingdom of God belongs."

Mark 10:14

This story of the parents bringing their children to Jesus
fascinates me! The disciples apparently think that Jesus' work is
"grown-up" stuff. They see the intrusion of "snotty-nosed kids"
as an interruption of something far more important. Jesus sees
it quite differently. Jesus helps us to "see differently," as well.

After the Maundy Thursday evening communion service,
Kaye and I took her car to pick up our children. Our son had a
baseball game and our daughter a baby-sitting job. Whether or
not to insist that our children always attend worship is a tough
issue for us. At a certain point, a "forced march" to church avails
little or nothing. As the children of two ministers, ours run the
double risk of the "preacher's kid" syndrome, which amounts to
a bad reaction to anything having to do with religion or the
church. So, for better or worse, we give them a fairly wide berth.
Faith cannot be imposed, but nurtured in the best ways we know
how.

On our way from rounding up the children, I decided not
to pick up my car, which I had left at the church. Instead, it
being a balmy spring evening, I was in a mood to walk back to
the church from home to retrieve my car. Having had little time
alone for weeks, I relished the prospect of a long, late-night
walk under the soft April sky. Maundy Thursday and the approach of Good Friday always touch in me an important spiri-

tual chord, bringing many reflections. Perhaps I would stay at the office and do a bit of writing. So, I set off from home for the two-mile trek.

My stride was just taking on a smooth rhythm and my tension being replaced by a pleasant thoughtfulness when Kaye pulled up beside me and tapped the horn. Our daughter jumped out of the car, her tennis shoes on. She had decided to join me for the walk. I checked the rising tide of irritation. My longed-for solitude had vanished!

As we walked together, I began to realize what a gift I had been given. Our children are in their early teens, a time of stress for them and us. I have feared these years when our children set their own courses, beginning to separate from parents and home in important but painful ways. A natural but disquieting distance opens up. Parent and child must now freely choose to reach out to each other, establishing a relationship on new ground. From here on, it is a matter of risk and freedom, desire and intention. Parenting at this stage cannot consist simply of shoring up structures and roles, but of becoming watchful for moments, openings. A fresh attentiveness and receptivity are needed. This was just such a moment.

We walked together through the warm evening, talking now and then about this or that, at ease in each other's presence. Before long, I found myself wishing that this moment would never end. As we rode home after picking up the car, I felt grateful that the evening I had planned for myself had been so graciously interrupted.

I Don't Get It!

For the message about the cross is foolishness
to those who are perishing, but to us who are
being saved it is the power of God....For God's
foolishness is wiser than human wisdom, and
God's weakness is stronger than human strength.
                              1 Corinthians 1:18, 25

One Lenten season I met with a group of mentally handicapped adults to prepare them for baptism on Easter Sunday.
Having these persons as members of our congregational family
is a blessing to us. They help us to live and to understand our
faith better.

The last session of our class fell on Good Friday. Our
congregation's prayer vigil began after the Maundy Thursday
service and continued until 3:30 p.m. on Friday. I suggested to
the group members that we take the final thirty-minute slot of
the vigil and then meet for our class. They were very agreeable.

On Friday, I picked them all up at the group home where
they live. As we drove to the church, I felt nervous, wondering
if this prayer vigil thing was a good idea. I talked with them
about how they might pass the half hour of silence, assuming
that such a long period of inactivity and prayer would be difficult for them to handle.

Once we were in the sanctuary, however, I learned a great
deal. Sitting together on the very front pew, the group quickly
settled into prayer and silence. I had pointed out to them the
large wooden cross on the chancel steps, explaining why it was
draped in black. Evidently this made an impression. After several minutes of silence, one of the women got up and walked

reverently to the cross. There she knelt and whispered a lengthy prayer. Soon the others followed suit, all kneeling, saying prayers, then quietly returning to their seats.

My initial response, out of my own nervousness, was to chuckle slightly to myself. How quickly this childish reaction faded as I realized the tenderness and, indeed, holiness of that moment. The question arose in my heart with a kind of gentle reprimand: "How long has it been, David, since you knelt, literally or figuratively, to pray before the cross?" Sure enough, in a moment I found myself following the lead of those I was supposed to be teaching.

A friend of mine is gingerly making his way back into the church after a period of disaffection. He is a thoughtful and spiritually sensitive person. His re-entry into the church is cautious, for he takes Christian faith and his commitment very seriously.

My friend has a delightful habit of grimacing slightly and saying, "I don't get it!" When up against a profound truth that he senses is essentially a mystery, his "I don't get it!" speaks for others who would like to be that honest.

In one conversation, my friend asked me to explain the crucifixion and why it is so important. After running through my understanding of the crucifixion as God's suffering love, bringing into play all the theological dexterity I could muster, I finally smiled and said wryly, "I don't get it either!" We agreed that there are some truths too deep for words, meant more, perhaps, to be lived than explained.

The crucifixion as God's saving love for all the world is not something one simply explains or ever fully understands. It is an event and the proclamation of that event. The crucifixion is not a problem to be worked out intellectually, though we need to seek fuller understanding to better express its meaning. Ultimately, the cross is a mystery of divine love upon which we fix our lives.

Kneeling before the cross that Good Friday, with my brothers and sisters in faith, I was in the presence of a great and gracious mystery that I may never "get," but that continues to unfold in my life in a challenging and powerful way.

And Especially Peter!

"But go, tell his disciples and Peter that he is
going ahead of you to Galilee; there you will see
him, just as he told you."

Mark 16:7

"Go, tell his disciples and Peter…." That's what the white-robed stranger in the tomb said to the awestruck women. Go tell his disciples…and Peter. Wasn't Peter also a disciple? Certainly he was! Then why did the messenger say so peculiarly, "…and Peter"?

The last time we saw Peter in Mark's Gospel, he was sobbing in the outer courtyard of the Sanhedrin. Jesus was inside, being interrogated. Peter had followed Jesus there after the dizzying, frightening scene of the late-night arrest. Peter stumbled along after Jesus, his chest heaving with fear and his head swimming in disbelief. Perhaps a scene from the recent past flashed mockingly into his mind. "Who do you say that I am?" Jesus had asked as they walked toward Jerusalem. Oh, Peter had been so bold and proud to burst out: "You are the Messiah of God, the Christ!" But then came Jesus' troubling words—he would go to Jerusalem, be rejected, suffer, and die. That's what Peter couldn't bear to hear. Don't talk of death and defeat when things seem to be in our favor and your popularity is growing! This will never happen to you, Teacher! It just *couldn't* happen! Then followed Jesus' stinging words of reprimand—Get behind me, Satan! You are not on God's side, but on the side of human beings (Mark 8:27–33). Perhaps, if Peter was recalling this, the same hot feeling of shame must have shot through him.

Now we find Peter in the courtyard, trying to blend into the landscape, to hide himself. And yet he just had to be near Jesus, frightened as he was of the dark forces threatening to engulf him as well. He ached to know the fate of his friend, his teacher. That's when he was noticed. Aren't you one of them? Yes, I believe you were with the man from Nazareth! Despite all his internal efforts, all he believed to be right and true and good, Peter's denial flew from his mouth. No! I am *not* one of them. I don't even know the man! Not just once, but three times came the denial. The very one Peter had loved so much, had tried so hard to understand, follow, and please, he had denied. Peter fled from the inner courtyard and collapsed in grief and tears.

That's where we last saw Peter. Peter, whose impetuous love for Jesus was his great gift. But also, he, the boldest of disciples, in the next moment could be so wrong, could miss the point so badly, could go out on precisely the wrong limb. Paul's words written decades later to new Christians trying to be faithful in their own difficult circumstances could have been written of Peter, as well: "I do not understand my own actions. For I do not do what I want, but I do the very thing I hate" (Romans 7:15).

Peter wanted so badly to be faithful, to do the right thing. He wanted to go with Jesus all the way, but he couldn't quite grasp what that way was. And when it came, it filled him with utter fear, freezing him in doubt and cowardice.

I think that in that early dawn hour, when the women were at the tomb, Peter was just where some of us are at times. Sunk in depression, beating ourselves because of failures. Seeing only the great gulf yawning between our lives as they are and what we thought they might be. Feeling despair because of our weaknesses, our inabilities to carry through the high resolve we once had.

Or…fearful because the glow of confident faith has faded in the face of the hard realities of the world, when evil seems more powerful than good, hate too compelling and even "sensible." In such moments, the love we thought was the salvation of the world seems no more than a wish-dream or so much pious fantasy. Or…feeling choked with guilt over what we've done or not done, having lost esteem in our own eyes because of this or that failure in our lives. Or…simply at our rope's end, the demands of living weighing too heavily, we feel powerless and ineffective. God now seems very far away, or not to exist at all.

If we've ever been where Peter was, in that damp, midnight courtyard, and for two days afterwards wandering in a desert of despondency, a haze of spiritual dryness, having given up on ourselves, on life, on God…then we are ready to understand the initially strange-sounding syntax of that Easter morning message. For this is the sense of the messenger's words: Go, tell his disciples…and *especially* Peter…he is going ahead of you to Galilee. You will see him there, just as he told you earlier. He is going on. Get up from your grief, your despair, your guilt, your hopelessness, your fear, your shame. It doesn't matter now. You can leave it behind. Get up and go, go to meet Jesus where he has gone ahead of you.

God is greater than our despair, greater than our feelings of shame or guilt, greater than our weaknesses and even our strengths. God is bringing new life. And God continues to call us on, into the grace of the new life that has dawned. Go tell *especially* Peter, because he especially needs to hear.

Do Not Hold on to Me

Jesus said to her, "Do not hold on to me, because I have not yet ascended to the Father. But go to my brothers...."

John 20:17

How skillfully the Gospel writers portray the resurrected presence of Jesus Christ! The resurrection defies direct and "photographic" description. This mysterious and profound event of God's power of new life must be pictured with great care, or else it will be rendered superficial and less meaningful.

In John's Gospel, Mary does not recognize the risen Christ. At first, she takes him for the gardener. Only when her name is spoken by her beloved Jesus does she know who he is. In speaking her name, Jesus reawakens the relationship of love between Mary and himself. She does not seek him; he seeks her. It is the risen Christ who calls our names and reveals himself to us.

Apparently Mary made a move to embrace Jesus out of her wild joy. Jesus has to ask her to let him go, not to hold on to him. His vocation is still not completed. He must ascend to God. Just as before, when Jesus told the disciples that they would understand everything he was teaching only after "his hour" had come, so now Jesus moves on in the further unfolding revelation of what God is doing in him. Mary is told to go and tell Jesus' disciples that he is ascending to "my Father and your Father, to my God and your God." This seems to be an echoing of the theme of Jesus' being lifted up so that all people will be drawn to God.

"And just as Moses lifted up the serpent in the wilderness, so must the Son of Man be lifted up, that whoever believes in him may have eternal life."

John 3:14–15

"And I, when I am lifted up from the earth, will draw all people to myself."

John 12:32

Mary must let Jesus go so that he may do his work. She cannot hold on to him, but she and the other disciples must go on to meet him where he is going, to follow him as he calls them and reveals himself to them.

What a different picture this biblical proclamation is from what we often hear today! Jesus is spoken of as a commodity that we can "have." "Put Jesus in your life!" So goes the kind of bumper-sticker Christianity that offers Jesus as a possession bringing us certain benefits. The biblical picture, however, is of Jesus who is not "possessed" but who possesses us, calls us forth, and leads us out of ourselves and into the life of service to others, the life of God's realm. In this nonpossessive following of Jesus, we find, paradoxically, that we are given true peace and joy.

The resurrected presence of Jesus Christ is not a reality we can hold onto. The Gospel writers understood that the reality and power of the resurrected Christ is experienced by us as we continue to follow him in faith and trust. Jesus is not to be "held on to" but "followed in faith."

Unless the Seed Dies

"Very truly, I tell you, unless a grain of wheat falls into the earth and dies, it remains just a single grain; but if it dies, it bears much fruit."

John 12:24

Spring is an ambiguous season. On the one hand, the earth is abundantly renewed. Returning warmth and color cast over our winter-weary spirits a mantle of vitality. To the "other hand" I will speak in a moment.

I was on a retreat at the Abbey of Gethsemani, near Bardstown, Kentucky, some years ago. The Abbey is Trappist, or Cistercian, a silent order. The rule of the guest house is also silence, with periods for conversation following meals. Sustained periods of silence allow the commotion of one's exterior life to settle so that the state of the interior life can be read.

The first day of my retreat I began to see how my mind had become full of a bundle of stresses and tensions that combined with physical weariness. I could not settle into reading yet, or any profitable reflection. The April afternoon was splendid, even summerlike, so I left my cubicle of a room, invading the woods and meadows of the Abbey property. Emerging from a stand of trees, I spied flecks of gold on the edge of a field in the distance. Shortly, I came into the middle of a carpet of jonquils. Standing in that sea of brilliant yellow and deep green, the sun bathing everything with warmth and light, I was powerfully moved. The delight I received from that lustrous patch of creation stood in stark contrast to my dark and knotted inward condition. There came a kind of healing in that moment, the sheer beauty mitigating my somber mood, a moment of grace.

Still, a jagged thought came to my mind: The earth is annually renewed, lavishly and faithfully, from the deathlike sleep of winter. But how are we renewed? When, in times of suffering and struggle, we sense that for us to live is always to experience death, the seemingly automatic transformation of the earth can seem more oppressive than comforting. How are we, who are so vulnerable to suffering and death, to gain hope and life?

This is the painful aspect, the "other hand," of spring's ambiguity. Psychologists tell us that for persons experiencing depression, April is indeed the "cruelest month." One sees all that beauty outside oneself, yet death and darkness seem to reign within. I think of the isolation from joy expressed in a painting by Paul Klee. The canvas shows a grid of black lines, like the bars of a prison, viewed from the inside. Through that dark grid can be seen a world of bright and varied colors, just out of reach. The title of the painting is *Outside Life Is Gay*.

Standing in that field of bright jonquils, my spirit felt greatly refreshed. Yet, still came the question: If you so clothe the jonquils of the field, O God, how do you clothe us, who feel the sting of human life, its vulnerability? How is it that we are not "crushed...driven to despair...forsaken...destroyed?" (2 Corinthians 4:8b–9).

In John's Gospel, Jesus is on his way to the cross, counseling his disciples to follow him, not in fear and dread, but in confidence and hope, even anticipation. Jesus talks with his disciples about what lies ahead of him, and them, should they follow. "Unless a grain of wheat falls into the earth and dies, it remains just a single grain; but if it dies, it bears much fruit." Jesus viewed his own dying as part of the process of new life. He does not oppose death and life as we do. There existed for Jesus a deep connection between the two. Jesus' "hour" of suffering is a moment that will give birth to new life.

A bit later, Jesus says to his disciples that their sorrow, like his own, will give way to joy. He likens this to the birth process. "When a woman is in labor, she has pain, because her hour has come. But when her child is born, she no longer remembers the anguish because of the joy of having brought a human being into the world" (16:21). I have heard women confirm this, that though they know the labor was difficult, that they felt anxiousness, even fear, they do not remember all of that as well as they recall the joy of birth. Suffering and joy, death and life are yoked together in a process of change toward new life, says Jesus.

The work of God in the crucifixion and resurrection has revealed to us this linking of death and life, suffering and growth. We are invited to live in this faith. None of it is automatic. No principle may be extracted here that makes everything pat and easy, a "sure thing." All remains a matter of faith, of moving into our darknesses, our times of struggle, trusting, sometimes through tears, that we will encounter God's presence there as the power of new life. The darkness, too, plays its part in God's grace.

Later in my retreat, sitting in the Abbey church, my soul was considerably quieter. One of the brothers walked to the lectern and read the lesson for that office. I had read and studied those same words often, probably preached on them many times. Now, however, I actually *heard* them as though for the first time:

> So if anyone is in Christ, there is a new creation:
> everything old has passed away; see, everything has
> become new!
>
> 2 Corinthians 5:17

Immediately came tears of joy and relief. I am in Christ, I thought. I *am* a new creation, already. I am pronounced new. How God sees me and how I see myself are vastly different. I am renewed not by my strenuous efforts to *be* something, but by God's grace alone that greets my struggles with growth, my experiences of death with new life!

Off in the hills, within a grove of pines in the Abbey woods, stand two pieces of sculpture. One you encounter as you enter the grove. There lie the sleeping disciples. The second figure becomes visible when you are in the very midst of that sanctuary of pines. There Jesus is on his knees, his face thrust to the sky, the palms of his hands covering his face in agonized prayer. In the sublime beauty of swaying pine trees and the spring sunlight filtering onto the floor of the forest, the anguished Jesus struggles to lay his sufferings in the hands of God, who, as the writer of the Letter to the Hebrews says, "was able to save him from death" (5:7b).

We, indeed, are renewed as is the earth. From season to season the earth receives new life. We are renewed by the faith we are granted in hours of struggle, the faith that opens our lives to the God of new life.

A Lesson in Limestone

So we do not lose heart. Even though our outer nature is wasting away, our inner nature is being renewed day by day. For this slight momentary affliction is preparing us for an eternal weight of glory beyond all measure, because we look not at what can be seen but at what cannot be seen; for what can be seen is temporary, but what cannot be seen is eternal.

2 Corinthians 4:16–18

An hour's drive south of Lexington, Kentucky, lies the Red River Gorge. This wilderness area consists of thick forests and cliffs that offer panoramic views. At the bottom of the gorge, a stream flows in and out of the dark green shadows. On various heights throughout the area stand arches of stone, with names such as Natural Bridge, Angels' Window, Sky Bridge. These arches are of limestone, the prevalent mineral in those parts.

The natural arches have been formed by the invisible hand of nature. Limestone is a pliable material in nature's hands. Rivers and rains, in partnership with the everconstant winds, have patiently and imperceptibly sculpted the face of the earth. When I stand in the presence of these arches, I am seeing the work of earth's most patient, most ancient artist—nature itself. To try to imagine the span of time represented by those graceful and delicate arches staggers the mind and humbles the spirit. Our lives are but a split second compared with theirs. We come and go; their beauty stays, as nature continues its shaping and reshaping.

I think how different we are from these monuments to time. They long preceded us and will be around—we hope!— for centuries to come. Paul's words echo in my mind: "...our outer nature is wasting away." We grow older. Our bodies begin to show wear and tear with years. The hairline recedes. A wrinkle here and there. We experience irritating little breakdowns that call for an array of appendages—bifocals, a hearing aid, an upper plate, arch supports. Mind you, all of this is not reserved only for those forty and over. Even the bodily awkwardness of adolescence is a sign of growing older as well as growing up.

Standing in the presence of a world that came before us and outlasts us, we see that even our best efforts to construct things that last crumble under the weight of years.

> For a thousand years in your sight
>   are like yesterday when it is past,
>   or like a watch in the night.
> You sweep them away; they are like a dream,
>   like grass that is renewed in the morning;
> in the morning it flourishes and is renewed;
>   in the evening it fades and withers.
> Psalm 90:4–6

Embracing an awareness of the transience of our lives is part of becoming truly human, as crushing as this knowledge may be at times. Paul writes, "Do not lose heart." But when our vulnerability, the realization of how short our years are, hits us full force, we want something to hang onto. We want to hide and play it safe, secure behind wealth or a sense of our "status," our comfortable notions about the world, reading only the good news, surrounding ourselves with friends who only confirm our own thoughts, values, and experiences. Life is risky and short! Better to play it safe and hold onto our illusions!

Our lives, of course, furnish us with plenty of experiences that cause us to want to flee into hiding. When my wife and I moved to Boston, Massachusetts, just after our marriage, we left the friendly and familiar landscape of the Virginia mountains and found ourselves in the midst of a large and strange city. Our apartment had no lock on the door when we first moved in. So while we waited for the landlord to fix it—three days we waited!—we figured that we should not leave the apartment unattended. One of us always stayed at home, protecting our sparse belongings from the hordes of thieves we were certain must have scouted us out by that time! Fear, suspicion, hiding. Even after the lock was in, for weeks we traveled only the shortest of distances possible, from home to work and back. All around us was a great city, full of interesting people and places, but our fear kept us from fully exploring it. After a few months, of course, the city began to become our home, and we could look back on those first days with considerable humor.

"Do not lose heart." Do not hide in fear. Do not shrink away from life, as fearful as it may seem. "Even though our outer nature is wasting away, our inner nature is being renewed day by day." Look at the limestone, says God. In a similar way, I am at work in you, shaping and molding you, from the inside out.

Paul does not say, "We are renewing ourselves day by day." The verb is passive. We are *being renewed*. We are being renewed in faith, which is the opposite of shrinking away. Faith is discovered and lived out in vulnerability, in risk, in openness to the shaping of God's Spirit as we live in the world. We are to hide neither from the world we are called to love nor from God in our self-pride and isolation. Rather, we expose ourselves to the buffeting winds of God's Spirit, sometimes working in bold gusts, sometimes in gentle breezes, and to the shaping waters of the world that suffers and at times brings us into suffering. When we follow this way, we *are* renewed every day, for God can then strengthen and guide us, and we can, without fear, live trustfully in a world filled with fear.

I once visited a congregation I had formerly served. This was my first visit back since leaving several years before. As I sat in worship, I felt an intense feeling of gratitude and love. I realized that my memories at that moment were all good! I did not remember the times of struggle, the conflicts, the low points—and there had been plenty! We—the congregation and I—had grown through those experiences. We had been shaped by our life together and by the sculpting presence of God's Spirit with us through it all. Somehow, I was a different, even stronger, person, because of those years. I would not have accepted such a possibility when in the throes of the more stressful times. I was older. They were older. Some had died. I would eventually die. The outer nature was certainly wasting away. But I could say in my heart that morning as I sat in that sanctuary, "Our inner nature *is* being renewed day by day."

Unlike the limestone, our lives are brief. Yet, like the limestone, shaped by the workings of nature, our lives, our spirits are shaped by the wind of God's Spirit, which grants us both steadfastness and change toward new life.

Pentecost
Ordinary
Time

The Bow of God

"When the bow is in the clouds, I will see it
and remember the everlasting covenant
between God and every living creature of all
flesh that is on the earth."

Genesis 9:16

One evening, following a dark afternoon of frowning clouds
and cold rain, the sun showed itself suddenly in a patch of clear
sky, just at sunset. Arching across the sky to the southeast appeared the most distinct rainbow I had ever seen. At the time, I
was heading for the neighborhood gas station with a nearly flat
tire. When I arrived, I found the attendant and a customer or two
standing in silent awe, drinking in the sight. It was as though the
whole city momentarily looked skyward. Of course, the Noah
story immediately popped into my mind—the "bow" of God set
in the clouds as a sign of the covenant, the promise never again
to bring destruction upon "all flesh." God's "bow of war" had been
set aside, hung up as a self-reminder of the divine promise.

In the flood story, the making of the covenant signals the end
of the fearfulness and deluge that have gone before. It is literally
the calm after the storm. Our delighted awe at the beauty of a
rainbow forms a correct response to the emotional tone of the
story. God set aside the bow of war, never again to rage over all
of life. The words of the spiritual, "gonna lay down my sword and
shield," apply to God in this instance. If God is to bring humanity
to a renewed life, it will be by other means than ravaging destruction. With this promise, God unilaterally pronounces peace. One
is reminded of the angels' song in the nativity story, when God
announces through them: "Peace on earth!"

For the ancient Israelite, there was yet a deeper meaning to the story. How come the world of nature is yet stable, a continuing blessing to human beings, in spite of human disharmony and violence? The Old Testament theologian Gerhard von Rad suggests that the answer embedded in the story is that the divine will is one of "healing forbearance." God sustains the world of nature, preserves that which God has given as a gift to humanity. All in all, the promise and the sign of that promise are intended to inspire and sustain faith that, in spite of extreme upheaval in human life, the world of creation remains constant. God will keep faith even if we do not. God yet intends peace although we continue to choose violence and war. Seeing God's war bow retired to its celestial place should turn us to the work of hanging up our human war bows as well.

The story of God's bow evokes the same faith and confidence expressed in Christian scriptures. (It is, after all, the same God!) Paul writes to the Roman church that, though we experience all manner of travail and chaos, nothing "in all creation, will be able to separate us from the love of God in Christ Jesus our Lord" (Romans 8:39b). The message remains the same: the fundamental tendency of life is toward life, not destruction; promise, not despair, peace and wholeness, not chaos and fragmentation. This is the work and promise of God.

Of course, that message may not always be heard by us or made as visible as the rainbow. But, once in a while, perhaps often enough, we are granted moments of looking skyward to see the sign. Mired as we become in our own violence, suffering, injustice, confusion, all of which seem to prevail, we are given sufficient glimpses of that which is able to sustain in us a certain and indomitable hope—God's sign of peace.

So he came and proclaimed peace to you who were far off and peace to those who were near; for through him both of us have access in one Spirit to the Father.

Ephesians 2:17–18

Single-mindedness

Jesus immediately reached out his hand and caught
him, saying to him, "You of little faith, why did
you doubt?"

Matthew 14:31

A curious thing happens to me now and again. In fact, it
happens all too often! Just the other day, for instance, I was
cleaning up in the kitchen after supper and had picked up the
trash to carry it outside. One moment I was headed outside; the
next, I found myself standing in the study, garbage bag in hand,
feeling ridiculous and thankful that no one was around to witness the event! What had happened? Somewhere on the way to
the trash cans, I started thinking about something else, unre-
lated to anything I was doing, one of the many thoughts that
float up and fix themselves suddenly in our minds, without in-
vitation.

Call it forgetfulness or absentmindedness. Whatever you
call it, this, I suspect, is a common human experience. We try to
think about two things at once. We schedule too many activities in one day and forget something. We try to do several tasks
at the same time. Or we simply get involved in a secondary
activity that draws our attention away from that which we had
planned or committed ourselves to do. It is all very frustrating,
very human, and at times very embarrassing.

In Matthew 14, we find the familiar story of Jesus walking
on the water in order to catch up with the disciples who had
gone ahead of him in a boat. He wasn't out to perform a miracle,
but to take a shortcut. The disciples are startled by the "ghost"
they spy coming at them across the lake. Jesus identifies him-

self. Then Peter, with characteristic impulsiveness and wanting to make certain it is truly his teacher, asks Jesus to let him walk on the water, as well. So, out of the boat steps Peter. He does very well...until his eye wanders! The churning waters snatch his attention and he begins to sink. In the end, Jesus pulls Peter out of the water. "You of little faith, why did you doubt?"

Now, what does doubt have to do with it? Isn't doubt an intellectual matter? "I *doubt* that Jesus was born of a virgin," or "I *doubt* that Jesus performed all those miracles." Even Thomas' doubt at the report of Jesus' resurrection has something of the intellectual about it (John 20).

The meaning of doubt in the story, however, is literally "thinking about two things at the same time," being double-minded. Doubt appears more as a matter of being distracted from the main thing, in this case, Jesus himself. As long as Peter keeps his eyes glued on Jesus, he is fine. Once his attention strays to those scary waves, he sinks.

Faith, then, would mean, in this case, single-minded attention focused on Jesus. Now, this is not a fanaticism that deliberately ignores every other reality. Single-minded faith is not the seeking of an escape from the turbulence of life, nor is it a lofty height from which to sit in judgment on everything and everyone. Walking amid troubled waters, with one's sight fixed on Jesus—this is faith.

> ...for in him all things in heaven and on earth were
> created, things visible and invisible, whether thrones
> or dominions or rulers or powers—all things have
> been created through him and for him. He himself
> is before all things, and in him *all things hold together*.
> Colossians 1:16–17 (italics added)

Doubt, then, does not have to do with harboring an intellectual reservation or being reluctant to accept certain points of theological doctrine. To doubt is to get distracted, to allow other things to take over our primary attention, so that we no longer walk with our eyes on Jesus, but on things that would overcome and paralyze us with fear, discouragement, or anxiety.

In the Civil Rights movement, some of the great slave songs and spirituals were enlisted in the cause. "Keep your hand on the plow, hold on" became "Keep your eyes on the prize [freedom], hold on." "Woke up this mornin' with my mind stayed on Jesus" became "Woke up this mornin' with my mind stayed on freedom." The words changed, but the meanings remained the same. To walk through the storm of racial hatred and oppression without being sunk by the waves, one had to keep a single-minded faith.

An ancient Celtic prayer beautifully expresses this notion of single-minded faith:

> Be the pain of Christ betwixt me and each pain,
> the love of Christ betwixt me and each love,
> the dearness of Christ betwixt me and each dearness,
> the kindness of Christ betwixt me and each kindness,
> the wish of Christ betwixt me and each will,
> and no venom can wound me.

A Dry and Weary Land

O God, you are my God, I seek you,
    my soul thirsts for you;
my flesh faints for you,
      as in a dry and weary land where there
        is no water.

Psalm 63:1

I recall one especially dry and hot summer. This was unusual for Virginia, which normally maintains such a moderate climate. The heat had cast an oppressiveness over spirit, mind, and body. Everything moved slowly. Making my pastoral rounds, I sought out the slightest shade in which to park the car so that it wouldn't be an oven when I returned. I cursed the day I decided to go with the more frugal un-air-conditioned car I drive. In my stuffy office, studying and writing were agonizing drudgery. My mind went to sleep and my body sagged. Extended heat waves bring out the worst in us. Tempers shorten. Impatient to get home to air-conditioned homes, we mutter at slow-moving traffic. Then, the kids want to go out to play, but I am too sluggish to manage it, now feeling both hot *and* guilty!

The heat punishes the poor the most, just as does the cold of winter. We remember the blistering summers of the mid-60s, when outrage over long-standing inner-city conditions and the heat of the summer sent people rioting and burning. Those who must endure the stifling heat in dark, hot apartments and inadequate housing, who suffer the indignity of unemployment, bear the worst. In such conditions, despair boils over into rage. Incidents of street and domestic violence increase.

Perhaps because of the prisonlike effects of midsummer heat, my mind plays a little trick. On the hottest of days, I find myself thinking of autumn—my favorite season—of the wind with a cooler edge to it, of putting on a flannel shirt for the first time, of the triumph of the earth's rotation over the worst of the summer inferno. In the midst of summer's blast, I get a mental foretaste of September.

The words of the psalmist come to mind—thirsting for God in a time when God's reality and presence are overshadowed, when the spirit is parched and longing. People of faith live by remembering and by foretaste. This does not mean that we escape the present—though we may wish to do so at times! Faith helps us to live in the present, dry as it can become, watered by remembering God and looking forward to the time when God's presence will again be known. Memory and hope go hand-in-hand for those who look to God.

There exists a spiritual dryness, when the sense of God's reality and presence flees. This "parched land" of the spirit often follows upon flushes of religious enthusiasm and zeal. It is a time of waiting, watching, and praying even when prayer is dry as dust. Some persevere through such times and come to greater, more mature faith. Others abandon the journey for the nearest oasis, though it may be found later to have been only a mirage. Some seek out whatever will yield a "religious experience," short-lived though it may be. After the first flush of joy at entering the church, we are faced with the realities of other human beings, all of whom are flawed and sinful. We then can either stay and come to a deeper experience of community, or leave in search of the illusory greener pastures, that is, a "better" church.

Spiritual dryness is a crucial part of faith, even an inevitable one. It is in such times that we discover what faith really is— trusting in, waiting for, living by God's word of promise and new life, when doing so doesn't come easily or even make much "sense." At such times, we remember what God has done, and we find in our very thirsting and hungering a foretaste of what God will do.

Complaining to God

Hear my voice, O God, in my complaint....
Psalm 64:1a

I arrived at the church early one summer morning that heralded yet another in a seemingly endless succession of days brutally hot and nights restless with thunderstorms. Once inside the church, I was met by the same old heat, as in an attic, mixed with the mugginess of the night's rain. I found myself, as in previous days, inwardly complaining about the weather and struggling to focus on the work at hand.

We complain much about the weather, and sometimes with good reason. There is, of course, our personal discomfort, but also the destruction extreme weather brings. Yes, we have reason enough for complaint. Now, the usual "religious" response to complaining is to utter something pious about being more thankful than sour-hearted. However, I would rather be biblical than religious in this case, for there *is* a difference.

A stroll through the Bible nets a host of complainers and complaints. Adam complained to God about "this woman" God had given him, wriggling out of his responsibility in eating the outlawed fruit. When God called Moses to liberate the Israelites, Moses immediately complained about the size of the job and the meagerness of his qualifications. Then, when the job was done, the newly liberated Israelites (you'd think they'd be grateful!) murmured at every turn about the austerity of life in the wilderness: "If only we had died by the hand of the LORD in the land of Egypt" (Exodus 16:3). And Moses complained to God about the "stiff-necked" people God had hung around his neck like an albatross. Moses even complained to God about

God, when God was ready to wipe them all out: "O LORD, why does your wrath burn hot against *your* own people, whom *you* brought out of the land of Egypt?" (Exodus 32:11b; italics added).

Elijah fled to the slopes of Mount Horeb because the message God had given him to speak had gotten him in hot water. When God asked what he was doing hiding out, Elijah complained about the dilemma he was in just for doing what God had asked him to do (1 Kings 19). Then, of course, there is the master complainer Jonah, who tried to evade the tough assignment God had given him. When God "repented" and didn't wipe out the contrary Ninevites, Jonah collapsed into jealous self-pity. His complaint was that God didn't do what God promised to do. Never mind God's mercy and compassion! God wasn't *consistent!*

In Christian Scriptures, the disciples are full of complaints. They complain because an "uncertified" teacher is doing things in Jesus' name and is stealing their thunder (Luke 9:49–50). Peter complains because Jesus insists on the suffering/crucifixion scenario for his messiahship rather than a more impressive warrior/king identity (Mark 8:31–33). When children are brought in on the "grown-up" business of Jesus' teachings, the disciples want them out of the way (Luke 18:15–17). And Jesus simply won't talk straight about things, using all those parables that make the disciples use their own heads. So they complain because Jesus makes things so hard: "Who can be saved?" Even Jesus does some complaining of his own, about hypocrisy and faithlessness he finds around him. His agonized complaint in the Garden of Gethsemane is: "Father,…remove this cup [of suffering] from me!" (Luke 22:42a).

Well, that's enough to show that when we complain, we stand in good company. Our complaining is not, of itself, an unholy act. In the biblical stories, the commiserations of God's servants are, we might say, the groans of those who carry the heavy load of being faithful to God in a tough world. The message seems not to be "Quit your griping!" but "Stay with it!

Keep your faith!" All this so that the servant, the faithful one, can say, "I kept on believing, even when I said [complained?], 'I am completely crushed,' even when I was afraid and said, 'No one can be trusted'"(Psalm 116:10–11, TEV).

Complaining may be only the sound of our humanity being converted to fuller life and faithfulness. God calls us beyond what we think are our limits in order to make us new people. Of course, we look to God to forgive our complaining. And when we complain, may our complaints be spoken to God rather than turned into curses. At the same time, in the heart of our complaint, we learn the language of thanksgiving, a deeper voice within us. This is the voice we want God to hear in our complaint. And always, we keep before us Jesus, who complained out of the depths of his suffering, and was heard by God who was able to save him from death (Hebrews 5:7).

Change My Brother!

"Friend, who set me to be a judge or arbitrator over you?"

Luke 12:14b

In this story from Luke's Gospel, someone in the crowd called out to Jesus: "Teacher, tell my brother to divide the family inheritance with me." The speaker wanted Jesus to step in and become an arbitrator. Jesus, however, saw a deeper issue in this sibling dispute over money.

If we stood in Jesus' place, we might be immediately drawn into the case. What are the facts? How can we settle things so that everyone has a fair share, so that justice is done? These are very appealing questions for us because we are eager to make things right. Children deftly lure their parents into sibling contests of will. Make my sister do this or that! It's not fair! We adults, too, nurse a strong sense of what is just, frequently carrying our causes to one another. Make this person do this or that! Look, I ask you, is this fair?

Jesus, though, dropped a bomb. He didn't get into the feud at all. He disowned the role of judge. "Friend, who set me to be a judge or arbitrator over you?" The man wanted Jesus to change his brother to suit him. Jesus would not cooperate. When life or other people don't suit us or go the way we expect, we complain and want things to change in our favor. So, too, might we come to Jesus or God with righteous petitions: "Change my brother, my sister!" "Change those other people and nations who don't think and act the way we do!" "Change this lousy world!" Our first response is to seek the solution not in ourselves but in the need for others to change.

"My purpose is not to change everything to suit you," Jesus seems to say. Then Jesus turned to the disciples and made an object lesson of this encounter. He didn't talk about what a bad deal this man was getting. He didn't generalize about the injustices of the world or other people's selfishness. He didn't side with the man's self-pity. He knew the nature of the wound in the man's life, and he knew, also, what was needed in order to heal it. He saw this man's compulsion to change his brother as the source of both his pain and his potential healing. Jesus would not change the man's brother, but he could help this man change himself in relationship to his brother, and to God. That is true healing!

Of course, there are situations and circumstances in the world that call for our active concern and intervention, things that most certainly need to be changed. Structures, systems, and values in our world inflict suffering and injustice, and stand in need of responsible Christian engagement. Jesus, however, opens up another, perhaps prior, area for our attention. To become a follower of Jesus Christ is to enter into one's own conversion.

To become disciples of Jesus Christ means to cease demanding that everyone else change. As disciples, we begin to discover ourselves as centers of God's dynamic, redemptive activity, which brings us into the life of God's realm. Jesus calls us away from "lording it over" others—"Change my brother!"—and leads us into true self-discovery through servanthood.

Jesus made this same point in other ways, at other times. Remember the story of Mary and Martha? Martha comes storming out of the kitchen, all irritated because Mary, her sister, sits with Jesus "doing nothing," while she is slaving away getting a nice dinner ready for their esteemed friend and guest. Change my sister! Make her come and help me get supper on the table! Jesus turns things around, however. He tries to get Martha to see that she needs to learn something about being more attentive to what really matters, about when to be active and when to be passive, listening, and learning. No, I won't change your sister, but I will help you change toward a fuller life. You can choose a different way!

Perhaps the most startling instance of Jesus' teaching along this line is his command that we love our enemies. Jesus says: I am not going to change your enemy or endorse your hostility toward those you consider enemies. I *will* help you change in relationship to your enemy so that you no longer respond out of a sense of threat, so that you become as a brother or sister to the one you regard as enemy.

These are hard words! Jesus calls us to be changed and changing people. He calls forth our capacities for change, and gives us the power of conversion, of new life, *metanoia,* repentance. What a joyful and liberating moment when we cease demanding that everyone else change and discover in ourselves the dynamics of our own conversion! What other meaning could there be in those often-read words from John's Gospel, "But to all who received him, who believed in his name, he gave power to become children of God"? (John 1:12).

What exactly was it that Jesus saw in this man that needed changing? He detected that the man was devoted to material things, and was a victim of the illusion that material wealth has something to do with fullness of life. Here lay the source of the man's pain. Thus, a story.

A farmer had a good year. It was such a successful year that he ran out of room to store all his produce. He built bigger and bigger barns. Wouldn't you know it? The rich get richer! He becomes further immersed in wealth and the care of his wealth. Then, when he gets it all laid up, he can sit back, relax, do some fishing, maybe take that dream vacation.

Then all of it collapses. Everything he so feverishly occupied himself with in the end provided no security at all. "You fool," says God. "Your life is at an end. What good are your barns bulging with surplus grain?" Jesus ends the story by saying that there are two ways of living from which we may choose—the way of laying up treasures on earth, or the way of richness toward God. The truly carefree life finds no security in having all we want or more than we need, but comes to us in Christ as we "become children of God" by God's gracious power.

For this man, then, the change needed in himself was his attachment to wealth, which stood as a block to his relationship to God and others. For us the issues may be different. But when we complain and bring our cases to God, pleading with God to change something or someone, we need to listen to Jesus saying to us, "No, I will not change your brother or sister. But I can help you change that in your life that is causing you to be alienated from God, others, and your true self."

Faithful persons are those involved in a struggle in their own spirits, to be converted from "change my brother" to that of "not my will but yours be done."

Service with a Snort

After sternly warning him he sent him away
at once....

Mark 1:43

When we approach this rather odd story of Jesus in Mark's Gospel, we must be ready to let go of our service-with-a-smile image of Jesus' compassion.

Jesus has just left Capernaum, more interested in keeping pace with his call to proclaim the realm of God than with healing all the people who flocked to him. "Let us go on to the neighboring towns, so that I may proclaim the message there also; for that is what I came out to do" (Mark 1:38). In this context, then, the leper rushes up to him: "If you choose, you can make me clean" (1:40b). What can Jesus do? He is trapped. A gauntlet has been tossed at his feet!

The text then says that Jesus was "moved with pity." Now, there exist other Greek texts of Mark that use a different phrase, not "moved with pity" but "filled with anger." That is quite a difference! Somewhere along the line in the development of this text, decisions were made in favor of a Jesus filled with pity rather than anger. Who would not prefer, after all, a service-with-a-smile Jesus to an angry and perturbed Jesus?

In the end, Jesus touches the man and makes him clean, physically and ritually, because lepers were also excluded from the ritual life of the community. We could, of course, make a sentimentalized meditation on the "healing touch of Jesus." A beautiful image, to be sure. However, what is the consequence of Jesus' touching this leper? Jesus has broken the law. In doing so, he has rendered himself unclean in the eyes of the establishment. Jesus must have known the consequences of his actions, that one who came in contact with a leper became as a leper in the eyes of society.

The leper's sudden approach and Jesus' forced response lend weight to the view that this whole scene was discomfiting for Jesus. The texts describing Jesus as angry may likely be the more authentic ones, after all.

The story, however, continues. "After sternly warning him he sent him away at once...." The word Mark uses here, translated "sternly warning," has a more graphic meaning—a noise made in a fit of emotion, like the snorting of a warhorse in battle. A Jesus filled with warm compassion could hardly be capable in the next instant of angrily snorting at the very one for whom he had felt compassion. Then Jesus "sends him away at once," a phrase used in the case of casting out demons. Jesus not only "snorts" at the leper but "casts him out."

The picture before us, then, is not of a gentle and mild Jesus, but a Jesus who seems to be at war with himself. If this is a story of Jesus' compassion, it is a peculiar sort of compassion, filled with self-struggle.

I wonder, however, if our own compassion is not also a matter of struggle? Most often, human beings must be interrupted by the needs of people and the world. We prefer our own agenda, our neatly ordered lives. When we are confronted by the pains, the suffering, the ugliness of life, we feel anger. Our idealized picture of things can no longer hold up. We must deal with the real world that presses in on us. We must respond, often feeling ill-equipped and unready to do so. If compassion is to have other than a sentimentalized meaning, it may be just this sort of struggle to respond to human need. We, too, become compassionate through much anger and snorting.

We see in this story the cost of servanthood for Jesus himself. To touch the untouchable results in becoming untouchable oneself. When white people reached out in solidarity with black persons in our country, denouncing the immorality of segregation and racism, great anger was stirred up. Those who stood beside their black brothers and sisters in the face of racism violated written and unwritten laws, and came to share, to some extent, the alienated condition of black Americans. Those in white churches who entered the struggle did so precisely in the context of Mark's story of the interrupted and angry Jesus. They felt compelled to touch the untouchable because of the gospel itself. They did not feel "ready" for it, as many were saying in those days, "We're not ready for change—go slowly!" We are never ready to deal with those things we wish to avoid, and compassion and justice are most frequently, it seems, wrenched from us.

It is of comfort, then, to see in Jesus what we feel in ourselves whenever we are forced to deal with the interruptive needs of the world. Struggle is a part of compassion, a part of living a meaningful life. Compassion is not easy! Jesus' own struggle is reassuring. He is in solidarity with us in our struggles for compassion. "For we do not have a high priest who is unable to sympathize with our weaknesses [struggles], but we have one who in every respect has been tested as we are, yet without sin" (Hebrews 4:15). The "without sin" could mean that Jesus, as in the case of the leper, was true to his calling, accepted the consequences of obedience, paid the price of compassion, embracing the anger and frustration it aroused for the sake of God's redemptive love and will.

Though Jesus "could no longer go into a town openly," the people began to flock to him. He would have other opportunities to get his message across, though many would not understand, concerned as they were only with their own healing, their own demons. Yet there was something new emerging, perhaps, in Jesus' reputation as a wonder-worker, a reputation he seems to have despised. He now was known as the rabbi who touched a leper. Some would understand what a profound expression of God's love this was, what a radical divestment of Jesus' own status had occurred, as he, too, became an outcast in the eyes of the world. People would glimpse another order of things, the new order of the realm of God.

American churches seem preoccupied with "bigness" and "growth." For the church to "touch" those who are considered untouchable in our society—HIV and AIDS patients and their friends and families, the homeless, gay and lesbian persons, the mentally or physically disabled—not in order to "do something" for them or to "fix" them, but to include them in the fellowship of Christ's community, might certainly be costly for the church. Such actions would forfeit the goals of bigness and success in favor of the struggle of compassion. Such a direction for the church's ministry would, in the end, speak most clearly of God's realm, which is like a great seine net thrown out broadly to gather in all people (Matthew 13:47–50).

Do Not Call Unclean!

The voice said to him again, a second time,
"What God has made clean, you must not call
profane."

If then God gave them the same
gift that he gave us when we believed in the
Lord Jesus Christ, who was I that I could
hinder God?"

Acts 10:15; 11:18

Kaye and I were interviewed by the religion writer of the local newspaper. She was writing a series of articles on the church and homosexuality. For a couple of years, we had opened up this topic with our congregation through sermons, study groups, and discussions. Here was an opportunity to raise another voice in the wider community, one of openness and charity, amidst the rising choruses of judgmentalism and condemnation.

For weeks afterwards we waited for the article to come out, not without a degree of anxiousness. Finally, the article containing our interview appeared in the Sunday paper. I hastily read it before leaving for the church, wondering what responses we would receive. Expecting the negative, I was encouraged to hear many positive remarks. I was especially moved by the words of appreciation that came from two of our older members, who thanked me after worship for what we had said in the article. One of these persons had spoken to me months before about the subject. For her there had been a personal dimension, which made her glad to hear the church speaking compassionately.

A differently poignant response came from a young physically handicapped woman in our congregation. As she shook my hand after the service, she looked at me intently and said, "People just don't know what it feels like to not be accepted."

I nodded, tears rimming my eyes. "But you know, don't you?" She gave a slight smile as she nodded in return.

Christian discussion and debate over homosexuality can either be open and productive, which seems rarely to happen, or subterranean and destructive, with people firmly dug into their positions. There is the added dimension of scriptural appeal, which lends the weight of the eternal and absolute to our finite human understanding and judgments.

The predictable recrimination is that God hates homosexuality because "the Bible says so." Scripture is read and used superficially, like an encyclopedia of ethics: What does the Bible say about this or that? Certain passages are cited uncritically and yoked with unexamined assumptions. All of this might seem only the curious phenomenon of religious discussion were it not for the prejudice and violence that are at stake. In the case of homosexual persons, incidents of harassment and hostility, even killings, are increasing in our society. There is something about homosexuality that touches the deepest of human feelings and fears. The matter cannot be resolved by quoting scripture.

I don't know how this will all come out. Perhaps homosexuality will become a great dividing issue for the church. "I came not to bring peace but a sword" are troubling words of Jesus. He spoke not of a literal sword, thereby lending weight to our warring impulses. Rather, he meant a metaphorical sword of division over what it means to be faithful to Christ and the good news of God's love. As slavery divided Christians in the last century, so might homosexuality divide the church today. Christian unity is important, even essential. Jesus prayed earnestly for the unity of his followers (John 17). Faithfulness to Christ, however, raises tensions, and may supersede the issue of unity, especially if our concern for unity masks a desire to avoid hard issues of human need and justice.

Whatever other issues there are regarding our homosexual brothers and sisters, such as human and legal rights, the church must realize that this is a matter of the heart. The power of inherited and embedded prejudices and hostilities holds us with an iron grip. Education, even legislation, cannot change the willful heart that does not want to be changed. How clearly we see this in the case of racial prejudice, decades now beyond desegregation laws but with racism still infecting our society.

In the lengthy but powerful story of Cornelius and Peter in The Acts of the Apostles, it took God's working with Peter at the deep level of a dream to change Peter's heart. How could Peter approach this Gentile, who was, moreover, a Roman soldier? Peter, thoroughly a Jew, with all the age-old feelings about "unclean" Gentiles! Through the dream that God sent to him, Peter learned in his heart about God's much wider grace and mercy. "Don't call profane what I have made clean," said God. Thus, from a changed heart and mind, Peter came to understand, as we must, that he could not stand as a hindrance to anyone or anything God had created and loved.

The Living Word

I will put my law within them, and I will
write it on their hearts; and I will be their God,
and they shall be my people.

Jeremiah 31:33b

One morning I was listening to a radio broadcast of a symphony concert. During the intermission, the famous conductor was interviewed. The discussion turned to the interpretation of the musical score. What this vintaged conductor said impressed me very much. Clarity and truth in interpretation do not come quickly, he said. It is not simply like learning to ride a bicycle. A young conductor is often expected to present a fully clarified interpretation after only a short period of study and practice. This is impossible! Some pages of Mahler—the composer of the just-performed symphony—are very clear to me now, he continued. Others are still quite cloudy. One cannot rush the process. It takes time and experience.

I thought about this for some time afterwards. Conducting or playing a piece of music can be done with technical precision but without understanding or feeling, without communicating the full texture of the music. With the maturity and experience of the musician, the musical presentation becomes fuller, clearer, more "truthful."

Is this not something like the life of faith, I wondered? Particularly when it comes to Scripture and its use and place in our lives? Knowledge of Scripture frequently means being able to quote the Bible with facility, matching every issue or question with a fistful of authoritative passages that seem to support one's point. On the other hand, Scripture is often approached as a kind of locked safe, yielding its "secrets" only to those having the right intellectual or spiritual acumen, who can decipher the combination. Thus there are those who are too facile in their use of Scripture as well as those who are too intimidated by Scripture.

The right place of Scripture, it seems to me, falls between the two, or perhaps even in a different place. We do not interpret Scripture so much as Scripture interprets us and our living. It does this by orienting us toward the "living word" of God. For the living word of God is not identical with the written words of Scripture, the writings of the faith community through the ages. The living word of God prompts and inspires Scripture. The word of God "spoke" creation into being. The word of God aroused in and through the prophets new understandings of God and life. The word "became flesh and lived among us" (John 1:14a). The Bible can arouse in us an attentiveness to God's living word through its words. Scripture directs our hearts, minds, and lives toward the living God who calls us to take the risks of faithfulness in today's world.

This is not to say that Scripture is unimportant and that our need to read and study it is diminished. Not at all! In fact, the opposite is the case. Scripture is to be "lived with" throughout our lives. The most faithful and dynamic way of appropriating Scripture is to live fully in the experiences of our lives while *at the same time* giving our ears to Scripture. There is thus a lively dialogue between Scripture and life, which gives birth to increasing understanding of faith and greater faithfulness to the living God. This, I think, is what God's words in Jeremiah mean: I will write my law on their hearts.

Like the wise reflections of that conductor, out of his many years of learning and practice, our lives of faith deepen with much faithful listening to Scripture and to life itself. In this way our "inner ears" become increasingly sensitive to God's *living* word in our own day and time.

No Thanks?

...rekindle the gift of God that is within you....
2 Timothy 1:6b

"...we have only done what we ought to have done!"
Luke 17:10b

This story of the dutiful servants in Luke 17 contains one of Jesus' hard sayings, one I have puzzled over for years. If you were the master, says Jesus, and you had a servant working in the field, and this servant came in from work—here's the question—would you sit the servant down and serve him dinner? No, says Jesus. "Do you [the master] thank the slave for doing what was commanded?" No. The servant serves, because that is *who* the servant is, seems to be the message.

Now, Jesus was not giving lessons on how to run an efficient household or advising how to treat servants so that they don't forget their place! Jesus taught something about the nature of faith and the life of faith. Initially, this story comes across as rather brusk, even offensive. Our first response may be mild shock. If the servant has been slaving away all day in the field, our sense of hospitality, even what we might deem a decent "Christian" instinct, would tell us that we should both serve a meal to this weary worker and express our gratitude.

While attending seminary in Lexington, Kentucky, I worked during the summers for my wife's uncle housing tobacco. The work was dirty, hot, and heavy, for this was burley tobacco—long, thick stalks and massive leaves. By noontime, since we had started at 7:30 in the morning and worked without letup, we were ready to sit in the shade of a tree and relish the sumptuous meal my wife's aunt brought out to us. What a treat to sit in the cool grass under a tree and be served fried chicken, green beans, potato salad, and iced tea! That's the way a worker should be treated!

But Jesus says something quite different. The servant does not expect to be served, but serves dinner to the master. The master does not even thank the servant, for the servant is simply doing what he is supposed to do. And when all is said and done, the servants—here Jesus seems to allude more directly to the disciples who serve God—simply say, "We are worthless slaves; we have done only what we ought to have done!"

I remember days when I would come home from work, tired from meetings, hospital visits, preparing sermons, writing letters, listening to people's hurt, anger, fear, and anxieties. I came home ready for a well-deserved break. Perhaps I could read the newspaper. Then, after having put my feet up for a while, I could finally sit down to a quiet family dinner.

But there was a problem with this plan of mine. My wife works as well. She would be coming home late. The children arrive home from school, bouncing with pent-up energy. They have their demands—Play ball with me! Take us to the store! Oh, yes...I remember that it is my night to fix supper. My head aches as I try to call up some residue of energy. It is the worst time of day, when one's energy is at its lowest and the demands of a two-career household are the greatest. I feel an undercurrent of resentment building. Doesn't anyone care to hear about *my* day? Why do I have to do all this? No one seems to notice, much less say "thank you." After resentment, I sink into self-pity.

We are used to being thanked. Gratitude is the proper and sensitive thing, to thank others and notice what they do for us. We enjoy being thanked, having our special efforts acknowledged. As children, we were taught to always remember to say "thank you" as often as we can. To appreciate others and their efforts that make life good for us feeds their spirits and gives them encouragement. It also reminds us of our need of others.

However, Jesus presses us to a deeper level of faith and living. For there exists a dark side to "thank you." We come to expect it, though we would be reluctant to admit it. We may even find ourselves motivated more and more by the recognition we expect to receive than by the nature of the task to which we've given ourselves. We have hungry egos, which grow hungrier, it seems, for recognition. Our spirits turn resentful when we are engaged in hard and demanding service to others. To give ourselves for others, as Christ taught and exemplified, drains us, takes something out of us. Despite our best efforts, we become discouraged, tired, and unhappy when we think we are not recognized for our efforts. How subtle is the temptation to live our lives with an eye always on what others will think of us, seeking their approval and admiration. The hungry ego never gets enough!

With this puzzling little story, Jesus probes the deeper meanings of faith. He calls us to the life-fulfilling path of self-emptying service. This is one of the chief paradoxes of the gospel: "For those who want to save [hang onto] their life will lose it, and those who lose their life for my sake, and for the sake of the gospel, will save it" (Mark 8:35).

Jesus' call to such a pouring out of our lives is not an arbitrary law laid down to see how miserable we can make ourselves! Instead, it is the path to the truly full and free life that flows from the death of the self, the transcending of the self, the life that shares in Christ's crucifixion and in the birth of the new self born in God's power. The seeking of recognition, the expectation of reward or acclaim remains a fixation on ourselves and not on God and our neighbor.

However, Jesus does not want us to become compulsive, neurotic people who inflict upon themselves endless activities in the name of selflessness, while seething inside with buried resentments. Jesus seeks our freedom, to liberate us from wrong motivations that detract from the love of God and neighbor. This calls for a deepening of our spiritual journeys, for deeper reflection and prayer. We need always to be opening ourselves up more and more to Christ's Spirit, without which we cannot receive this gift of new life that shows itself in self-emptying love.

When we give ourselves for others, when we are involved in being there for another human being, making that person's well-being our highest priority, we experience a "losing of the self" that renews us, that puts us in touch with the very life of God—love. The loftiest moments occur when we have been drawn beyond ourselves into the place where God meets us in the life of another human being. It is then that we have touched upon our true identities, which come to us not by endlessly examining ourselves or focusing on our own lives, but by going out of ourselves for others. This experience of liberation and new life awaits all who follow Christ's call into servanthood. As we walk that path we rediscover who we really are and are meant to be by the God in whose image we were created.

What? No thanks? We don't really need it, for we are fulfilled as we *are* ourselves in Christ—servants. Our example is Jesus, who knew who he was, and, knowing that, gave his life for us and the world.

> Jesus, knowing that the Father had given all things into his hands, and that he had come from God and was going to God, got up from the table, took off his outer robe, and tied a towel around himself. Then he poured water into a basin and began to wash the disciples' feet....
> John 13:3–5a

God's Affirmative Action Plan

I will seek the lost, and I will bring back the
strayed, and I will bind up the injured, and I
will strengthen the weak, but the fat and the
strong I will destroy. I will feed them with
justice.

Ezekiel 34:16

The phrase "affirmative action" has gotten people all stirred
up in recent years. When federal programs were implemented
to benefit the poor, persons of color, women, the disabled, and
so forth, giving them a perceived edge over white, middle-class,
able-bodied males, the cries of "Foul!" resounded through the
nation.

The idea of affirmative action functions on the premise that
certain people and classes of people have had the "edge" taken
from them for a long time, if they ever had it at all. There is
some catching-up to do in order to help these persons share
equally in an affluent society. However, when such programs
and guidelines were implemented, some saw what they called
"reverse discrimination" because place had to be given to others, sometimes *their* place! We are a democratic society, went
the objection, and everyone must be treated equally, not given
preferential treatment.

Needless to say, affirmative action has had a rough road. It
seems extremely difficult for a nation to act out of a national
conscience for the benefit of groups within it. Many people cannot sustain a morality that pays particular attention to those
who have been wronged in the past, especially when it means
self-sacrificing actions.

I find affirmative action thinking to be highly resonant with Jewish and Christian scriptures. But it remains as tough to handle there as in the context of our current society. When we read through the prophets of Israel, we find God paying particular attention to certain people—the blind, the lame, the sick, the poor, the powerless, the forgotten. In Ezekiel 34, God announces that divine personal attention will be given to the matter: "I myself will search for my sheep...I will seek the lost...I will bring back the strayed...I will bind up the injured...I will strengthen the weak....I will feed them with justice."

Ezekiel denounces, on God's behalf, the false "shepherds" who have fed themselves and not the flock (34:2). The "good life" has become the private property of those who can afford it. Those who cannot are simply left to get by on their own. "Let them pull themselves up by their own bootstraps!" The appeal to "self-sufficiency" or "self-help" can serve as a handy dodge, keeping us from seeing the systemic problems that keep people in poverty and the despair that poverty brings. Such avoidance also helps those of us who are privileged to deny that we may be part of the problem, that our own self-sufficiency is in large part a product of our privileged position. The true shepherd, like the Chief Shepherd—God—has special concern, however, for those who are left out. They are not left to their own devices.

God's action sets out to right past wrongs, even at the expense of those who now enjoy comfort and privilege. God's justice is not blind, but looks closely to see who suffers. God indeed takes sides, is not impartial when it comes to people's sufferings. Ezekiel's message is that God is taking charge with an affirmative action plan of divine love and justice.

The justice of God *is* God's compassionate love moving into action. Compassion is love particularly focused on those in need. There exists no superficial pity here, no one-time love gift given to soothe the uneasy conscience. The serious work of righting wrongs takes the determination and sacrifice of God's will working through us.

Central to this divine affirmative action plan is our realizing that God has so dealt with each and all of us. For Israel, the memory of the Exodus was of critical importance. "Remember that you were a slave in the land of Egypt, and the LORD your God redeemed you; for this reason I lay this command upon you today"(Deuteronomy 15:15). What God commanded had to do with caring for the poor, the sojourner (resident alien?), and the servant (15:4–14). For Christians, the matter includes the Exodus as well as the "new Exodus," the cross of Christ. We have tasted God's special favor, God's particular love for those in need. In the First Letter of John, this is expressed so: God has loved us, so we are to love one another. What God has done for us becomes the basis for our actions toward others. We are to love as we have been loved.

For people of faith, much is at stake. How and where do we experience God? How and where do we find God's love and light? In Isaiah 58, Israel's light and life emerge when judgmentalism and accusation are eliminated, as people pour out themselves for the feeding of the hungry and the freeing of the oppressed. "Then your light shall rise in the darkness and your gloom be like the noonday" (Isaiah 58:10b). In Matthew's Gospel, Jesus closes his teachings with a lengthy parable of the "great judgment."(25:31–46) Some find themselves before the Son of Man receiving blessings because they fed the hungry, clothed the naked, visited the sick, and otherwise paid special attention to the status of their brothers and sisters. Others, however, find condemnation because they saw it all, but did nothing. Why is this so? Because Jesus identifies himself with those who are ministered to or not. It was as the "sheep" went about affirmative action living and loving that they "did it unto" Jesus, not even conscious that they were doing so.

The good news of God's redemptive love confronts our conventional thinking about what is fair and just. The realm of God has to do with the last becoming first, the least greatest. For those who live in expectancy of that realm, the reordering of life on behalf of the "least" and the "last" constitutes both the blessing and the challenge of God's affirmative action love.

Inconvenience and Suffering

"There was a rich man who was dressed in purple
and fine linen and who feasted sumptuously every
day. And at his gate lay a poor man named
Lazarus...."

Luke 16:19–20a

The following story tells of one day in my life that taught
me the difference between inconvenience and suffering.

That morning I was to visit a young mother whose eight-
year-old daughter had full-blown AIDS. This family was re-
ferred to me by our hospice organization.

On the way, however, I had an errand to run. I needed to
deliver some information to a woman in the local poetry society
who had asked me to perform some folk songs for the fall meeting.
I found the house easily and coasted up the driveway beside her
home. As I dropped the envelope through the mail slot, there
being no answer to the doorbell, a late-model station wagon
pulled up aggressively behind my car. I then realized that in my
joy at finding the right house so quickly, I had entered the wrong
driveway. I walked toward the car, composing my apology.

Out of the station wagon stormed a well-dressed woman
considerably younger than I. Her firm stride signaled that I was
"in for it." At that moment I noticed another person getting
out of the wagon, an older black woman dressed for house-
work. Many well-situated white residents in our city employ
black "help" in their large homes. So, one sees the familiar sight—
prim upper-middle-class white women driving their black "help"
up to their overspacious homes. They get a great amount of
work at a very "reasonable" cost.

"I am sorry," I said. "I didn't realize this was your driveway." I received an icy look, intended to put me in my place. "This happens all too often," she snapped. I felt anger rise in my chest as I realized I was being dressed down by a woman considerably my junior. "It is *very* inconvenient!" I assured her I would right the wrong immediately and move my car. With a final assertion of her authority, she spat out, "Good!"

I backed onto the street and was thankful to be on my way, yet feeling dislocated. As I drove toward my original appointment, my head swirled with thoughts. This young woman's arrogance and sense of outrage at being inconvenienced stood in bold contrast to the situation of true suffering that awaited me.

Minutes later I sat in the small living room of a modest apartment with a mother slightly younger than the woman I had just left. On this person's face were written volumes of weariness and strain. Her daughter had been very sick the night before and could not go to school. Two other children were there, as well, being tended for a little extra income. So, with the children buzzing about, our conversation was frequently interrupted.

At one point, during a lull in the children's activities, I asked this young mother what help she needed most. Her face came alive with grief and searching. What she needed most, she responded with a shaking voice, was help in facing her daughter's death. My mind reached back to the years I had worked at Boston Children's Hospital prior to seminary. My first experiences with death were with children and the singular pain experienced by their parents. A great cavern of grief swallows up quick answers or facile words intended to soothe. What can be said to a mother facing the death of her child? I assured her that I and the church would be there for her, walking with her through the valley ahead. In a situation where too much can be said, this seemed to be enough.

These two encounters remained vivid in my mind. A woman whose greatest worry seemed to be the abuse of her driveway by an unsuspecting intruder. A mother facing the death of her daughter. A great chasm lay between those two women, similar to that which yawned between Lazarus and the rich man in Jesus' story. The tragedy of the story is that the chasm became unbridgeable after death. Reaching across the spaces between us this side of death can be the most holy and healing work we can be about. I thought: the first woman really needs to meet the second. We can experience considerable healing when we distinguish between what is inconvenience and what is truly suffering.

Two Kinds of Poverty

"Blessed are the poor in spirit, for theirs is the kingdom of heaven."

Matthew 5:3

"Blessed are you who are poor,
    for yours is the kingdom of God."

Luke 6:20

Two photographs came to my attention in the same week. In the newspaper there appeared a curious picture of a woman holding up a sketch of her lost dog. She was offering a reward of several thousand dollars for its recovery. The accompanying story told of the thousands of dollars already spent by the woman and her husband for publicity in their search for the beloved pet. Here was, I thought, an example of flagrant affluence. I, too, have a beloved pet, but could never persuade my conscience to allow me to offer such a sum, even if I had it!

The other photograph was one of several in the *Time* magazine coverage of famine and starvation in Sudan, caused by brutal civil war. Crawling across the page of the magazine was a grown man who looked like a moving skeleton, looking hopelessly for food.

What a contrast! How can our world yield both these pictures! What is it in our world, in us, that makes these pictures possible? As a middle-class U.S. citizen and Christian, I live between these two pictures, these two realities. They question me, and unless I numb myself to their witness—one of wanton affluence, the other of wanton inhumanity—I must struggle with the connection between them. More than that, I must respond somehow in my own life to these two "words" spoken to me about our world.

My dilemma was put into a helpful perspective through a subsequent experience.

One Sunday afternoon I paid a visit to D— and his wife and child. They are refugees who had been resettled in the city by our congregations. I am in awe of such persons who come into a foreign society, facing mountainous obstacles of language, economy, culture. D— has come a long way in a short time, displaying remarkable discipline and courage. He and his wife are amazingly focused on making a go of it here.

When I walked into their apartment, I felt welcomed and at home. Because of limited income, D—'s family had to settle for a damp basement apartment in a dilapidated house. But D—'s wife has added her own touches, making it feel very homelike.

I was ushered into the living room as D—'s wife exited to make coffee. I was so mindful of their relative poverty that at first I was reluctant to accept their offer of refreshments. Then I quickly realized this would be a rejection of their hospitality.

D— and I talked. He is a slender man in his early thirties. His face changes in complete conformity to his inner moods.

His eyes are bright and honest. Here is a man who is in touch with the realities of his life, his struggles, but also his strengths. He tells me of his difficulties with this culture. Particularly he is annoyed by people's habit of smiling all the time, even when the smile is not genuine or especially appropriate. He cannot do this, though he feels like it is part of the game of getting ahead. I liked this observation very much, and admired D—'s honesty.

I stayed for over an hour. During the visit I learned more about D—'s life: how he escaped from the political dictatorship of his homeland, but not before he was imprisoned and tortured; how he witnessed the execution of a friend; the eight years he and his wife lived in a refugee camp.

I left that apartment feeling strangely renewed and hopeful. My ministerial work takes place largely with middle- and upper-middle-class people, which includes myself and my family. Over the years, I have come to recognize the impoverishment of spirit (different from "poverty of spirit") that accompanies affluence. It is hard to hear the gospel when what concerns us most is having a bigger house, a newer car, securing higher incomes, or having clothes that make us appear respectable and influential. It is hard to hear the message of self-sacrificing love when we are unwilling to forgo at times a meal in a restaurant or a vacation at the beach for the sake of giving more to those who are in need. It is hard to hear the message of God's grace when we are caught up in building our own status, progressing up career ladders, and generally consumed by our own interests.

The Beatitudes in Matthew and Luke are not commandments or laws. They are pronouncements of blessing, God's blessing falling on us in circumstances we usually don't think of as particularly "blessed." Poverty of spirit is an openness at the center of our being for God alone, an "emptiness" that is filled only by God. Material poverty might mean for us who are affluent lives less full of things and preoccupations that detract from what truly matters. Both kinds of poverty beckon us, for in them, God calls us into blessedness. If we as a human family cannot progress in these Beatitudes, cannot receive these blessings, then the two realities represented in those photographs will continue to grow in our world.

For me, blessing and struggle go hand-in-hand. I was encouraged in both by my friend that Sunday afternoon.

Rooftop Experiences

When the LORD descended upon Mount Sinai, to the top of the mountain, the LORD summoned Moses to the top of the mountain, and Moses went up.

Exodus 19:20

Some people have "mountaintop" experiences. Psychologists speak of "peak" experiences, times when a person's life becomes especially full of meaning.

Mountains, peaks—but I think, however, of my "rooftop" experiences. Don't get me wrong. I love mountains *and* peaks. It's just that I've found myself on rooftops nearly as often as on mountaintops. Once, I spent my day off painting the porch roof of an old house my wife and I were trying valiantly to rehabilitate. A porch roof sounds modest, but ours was a gigantic inner city house, and this particular roof was as large as most main roofs. The day was splendid, with brilliant sunshine and a grand sky. The late summer heat was made bearable by an intermittent breeze spiced with a hint of autumn. Summer insects made their summer noises in the branches of a massive oak that stood beside the house. My radio, perched precariously on a window sill, offered up a favorite Sibelius symphony that I had first heard as a college student. My head was filled with pleasant thoughts of past and recent events in my life. And I was enjoying the painting, as well. Like others whose work consists mostly of mental or interior exertion, I find that manual labor offers a refreshing counterpoint. When my hands are busy, also, my mind is set free to dance over many and varied thoughts. Thus, my "rooftop" experience.

Perched on my roof, brush in hand, I tried to reflect biblically on rooftops and their meanings. Alas, rooftops do not play a prominent role in scripture, although David did spy Bathsheba on her rooftop from his. At one point, my neighbor, Valerie, peered out her second-story window to say something unintelligible to me. Like Bathsheba, she was unadorned—in her three-year-old sort of way! Then there was Jesus on the pinnacle (rooftop?) of the Jerusalem temple being tested by Satan. "Throw yourself down and let the angels take care of you!" Jesus refused the heroics in favor of whatever God, not Satan, would ask him to do, grand or small. I was not in the least tempted to cast myself off my roof, but for less noble reasons. Then there were the friends who resorted to rooftop tactics in order to get their paralytic companion close enough to Jesus for the great rabbi to heal him. But theirs was a situation of pragmatics—the roof as a means to an end. My roof-sitting was rather an end in itself, affording a certain panoramic view of my life.

Another thing, however, about mountaintops and rooftops—we are not meant to stay there. Moses goes up Mount Sinai to receive the laws of the covenant, a covenant to be lived out, not on a mountain, but on the plains of daily life. God tells Elijah to get off Mount Horeb, the holy mountain, and return to his proper work as a prophet (1 Kings 19). Elijah was using the mountaintop as an escape—a permanent one, he hoped! But from God's point of view, Elijah's business was not up on the mountain but down among the people. Jesus takes the disciples up on a "high mountain," and there he is transformed in front of their eyes (Mark 9; Matthew 17; Luke 9). Peter, in essence, wants to camp there for a while and enjoy the divine serenity of it all. However, the disciples are meant to stay up there only long enough to hear God confirm Jesus as the one to whom they must listen. Such mountaintop moments are important, even necessary, for us to glimpse periodically the deeper realities of life. But they must serve, in the end, to enable us to live more fully on the level ground of everyday life.

There do come to us those moments—mountaintop, rooftop—when we take a deep breath and are glad to be alive, when we are, even for a short while, at peace with life, open to beauty, and quietly, profoundly grateful for our lives. In a day when we fall prey to the temptation to manage and manipulate life, when we become crippled with stress in our efforts to be "in charge" and to "get ahead," we would do well to cultivate a capacity for receiving life as a gift. We have plenty of time for worry, stress, anxiety, and for taking up the important responsibilities of our lives. But to "ponder the lilies of the field," be it from rooftop or mountaintop, is a thing we dare not deny ourselves.

We Have an Advocate

If we say we have no sin, we deceive ourselves, and
the truth is not in us....My little children, I am
writing these things to you so that you may not sin.
But if anyone does sin, we have an advocate with
the Father, Jesus Christ the righteous....

1 John 1:8; 2:1

Some years ago I was attending a peace conference at a small
college in Kentucky. The assembly hall being filled by the time
I arrived, I located a spot on the floor at the back. I had just
settled in and was beginning to focus on the proceedings when
I felt a hand on my shoulder and heard a voice: "Will you be my
advocate?" I turned to see a young man with a physical disability, leaning toward me on his crutches. It was not the disability
that made me hesitate in my response, but his question: "Will
you be my advocate?" My hesitation betrayed my confusion,
and the young man saw that I needed a translation: "Would
you please help me find a seat?" Relieved, I set about locating a
chair for him.

After he was seated, I returned to my place. For a long time
I could not concentrate on the meeting because my mind lin-
gered over the meaning of my new friend's request. Since that
day, I have learned that *advocate* has a special meaning in the
world of disabilities. On the face of it, I was simply being asked
to find this person a seat. Yet, to be asked to be someone's advocate has a different, deeper shade of meaning. A special sort of
relationship is called forth.

To be an advocate means far more than helping persons get
around or doing something for them that they are unable to do

for themselves. An advocate is not simply a helper, an intercessor for persons with disabilities. The advocate is called upon to *represent* the person in the world, and to represent that person, *not* in order to gain sympathy or to stand in the person's stead, but to say, "This person is valuable, has integrity, and is essential to us." In short, an advocate does not regard the person as "disabled."

So, being asked to be an advocate and to get a chair for someone can really be two quite different things, the first far weightier than the second. The advocate is not simply asked to do something for someone—indeed, may be asked *not* to do something *for* someone—but to hold a particular viewpoint toward that person.

The writer of 1 John speaks of Christ as our advocate. Why do we need an advocate? Because we share a common, universal disability—our failure in the love of God and one another: that is, sin. Though we are, in Christ, called to sinlessness—the life of love—when we do sin, we have someone on our side. The upshot is that we are all disabled. There are not sinful and sinless people, the handicapped and the unhandicapped. "If we say we have no sin, we deceive ourselves, and the truth is not in us." Our disability in love persists, even though we now live in the community of Christ. To say we know Christ—that is, that we have communion with him—and to live in the way of love to which he calls us can be very difficult for us to integrate. God's advocating grace in Christ bridges the gap.

At a youth group meeting one Sunday evening, I sat with a group of teenagers. We discussed our attitudes toward persons deemed handicapped. One young man straightway shared his thought that we all have handicaps. A sensitive and wise insight! All of us have or develop handicaps of one sort or another: something, some experience, some wound that leaves us less than whole, unable to live fully.

That is why we need an advocate. The word the writer of 1 John uses is *paraklaytos*, the same word used by Jesus when he speaks of the Holy Spirit coming to be with his followers (John

14:26). Here, the writer says that Jesus himself is our advocate. Just how does Jesus fulfill this role for us?

First, Christ *is* God's forgiveness in our lives. Forgiveness constitutes the way God's love comes to us, removing the obstacle of our sinfulness. God in Christ comes to us "not counting [our] trespasses against [us]"(2 Corinthians 5:19b). How can we describe this dimension of God's relationship to us except as grace, a gift? In God's love for us, our failure in the life of love, which we experience as immovable by our own strength of effort, is removed by God, put aside, covered over. This is Christ's advocacy of us. We who are disabled in the life of love are regarded as able-bodied, are treated as whole, without regard to our disability.

Here, already, is the second point. We are, in Christ, made able. In Christ, we are perceived as we truly are, creatures of God, created with the capacity to live in communion with God and one another. We might say that in Christ, God comes to us perceiving us according to our true selves, the image of God in which we are created. And this when we can no longer see it ourselves, when we have lost a sense of who we really are. The disability—our sinfulness—is a distortion of that *imago dei*, and is disregarded and broken through by God's love. Now we can understand Paul's words of profound joy: "If God is *for us* [our advocate], who is against us?" (Romans 8:31b, italics added).

What people with physical or mental impairments need most is not, first of all, for someone to do something for them. Least of all do they need pity or our subtle, even unconscious feelings of superiority that breed patronizing attitudes and actions. What such persons do need is for us to have a clarity of perception, seeing them as individuals, human beings who are loved by God, with gifts to offer, with the same humanizing rights and responsibilities as anyone else. What is needed is an empowering relationship—advocacy.

God sees us as whole even when we are not whole. God pronounces us righteous at the same moment we feel unworthy. If this is the way God loves us, then we also are to love each other in that same way (1 John 4). We are made able, because of God's prior love for us, to be advocates for one another, regardless of our disability, our sin, our woundedness. In this way, we see one another with the eyes of God.

Free to Suffer, Free to Live

Although he was a Son, he learned obedience
through what he suffered....
                                    Hebrews 5:8

While living in Boston many years ago, Kaye and I worked at Boston Children's Hospital Medical Center. As a conscientious objector, I had two years of civilian service to perform. So, I worked as an orderly on the cardiac medical and surgical division at Children's.

Early on in my work, I learned an unflattering term frequently used by the nursing staff, only among themselves: *cardiac cripple*. A "cardiac cripple" was a patient who had been so overprotected by parents that he or she could not function independently. Such patients were often emotionally "clingy" and given to complaining and whining. The result of such overprotection was low self-esteem, thus little self-confidence.

One young man, however, stood apart from others who fell into the "cardiac cripple" category. Sonny was nineteen years old. He had been in and out of the hospital all his life, had undergone several operations, lived with the aid of a pacemaker implanted in his chest, and had every physical reason not to be alive. Sonny should have been a prime example of the cardiac cripple syndrome.

However, Sonny held a part-time job painting sailboats and led an active social life. Whenever we heard he was coming onto our division, we all perked up. Sonny brightened the whole place with his impish smile, practical jokes, and incessant kidding of the nurses.

What made Sonny so different? The interest of the nursing staff was piqued. Far more than simple curiosity, however, we wanted to find out from Sonny's situation something that would help us work with other patients and their families. So, we invited Sonny's mother to attend one of our patient care conferences so that we could talk with her and learn Sonny's "secret."

All I remember from that conference is a story that Sonny's mother told, and, as it turned out, that was all we really needed to remember.

When her son was quite small, Sonny's mother watched him one day from the kitchen window as he played in the backyard. All at once Sonny began racing toward the back fence, intending to heave himself over it. Knowing full well her son's fragile condition, she saw the danger. Such exertion could kill him in an instant. She made a move toward the door to scream out for Sonny to stop. Instead, she sat down at the kitchen table, and cried. In that excruciating moment, she understood that this would be the way things had to be if her son was to live a full life, though it may be a brief one. At a profound depth in her being, she let her son go into the dignity of his own life.

Perhaps most people would have been horrified at what they judged to be this mother's endangering of her fragile son. As I recall, however, those of us in the conference that day felt a speechless wonder. We had learned something vital about risk, about life, about freedom, and finally about the true nature and cost of love.

God's love for Jesus did not take away from him the suffering he faced. Instead, "he learned obedience through what he suffered." I think this means that Jesus learned the saving intimacy with God that comes through trust. He learned this as he entered fully into the calling of his own life. God did not rescue him or protect him from life, but was with him. In the end, God gave him fullness of life.

God does not remove from us our sufferings and struggles. When we keep our lives open to God in the midst of those very struggles, we learn, as did Jesus, the faith that keeps us from being completely overwhelmed. And we are led into fuller and freer lives.

Loving one another with this same love with which God loves us, we grow to understand that we do not belong to each other in a way that prevents freedom. Out of the most caring of motivations we may seek to protect others—our children, our friends, our spouses. But in doing so, our actions often take from others the very freedom God has given them. Without realizing it, we have stepped into God's place, interjecting ourselves between others and God. It is one of the subtlest and most challenging of tasks to love others in ways that preserve the dignity and freedom they have from and in God.

A Messenger of Grace

I met Robbie when he was admitted to our unit at Boston Children's Hospital. Robbie was dubbed a "problem patient." He was a large, even obese, Down's syndrome boy about twelve years old. As I was the only male on the nursing staff of our division, the charge nurse assigned Robbie to me. I accepted the assignment with a half-jesting remark about female chauvinism. Since I was male, it was assumed I had the best chance of handling Robbie!

The first few days of Robbie's hospitalization witnessed one stand-off after another. I would attempt to take Robbie's vital signs; he would jerk down his gown to prevent my listening through the stethoscope. I managed to get his blood pressure only after long periods of strategizing and cajoling. Every attempt to get these things done was greeted by his obstinate grunt—"Unh-uh!" And every overture at friendship on my part was rebuffed.

The greatest challenge came the day I was to take Robbie to radiology for X-rays. Somehow he got wind of it, and when I entered the room with the wheelchair, Robbie had barricaded himself in the tiny bathroom. Through a contortion that was truly amazing, he had lodged himself under the sink! Dislodging him called for the efforts of several of us. At last Robbie was begrudgingly on his way. Once I regained my composure and my breath from the struggle, I chuckled to myself as I wheeled Robbie along the halls. I was beginning to feel a deep affection for my obstinate charge!

A breakthrough came, however. One morning after I checked in, I began the rounds of my patient assignments. As I entered Robbie's room, he was sitting in the middle of his bed, Buddha-like, with his legs crossed in front of him. He watched me out of the corners of his eyes. As I rounded his bed, he deftly reached out and snatched my stethoscope from my hip pocket. My first impulse of irritation gave way to utter delight. There sat Robbie, hiding my stethoscope behind his back with a huge smile on his face. We had made it, Robbie and I! After days of effort, sparring, testing, we had found the common ground of friendship.

It was spring in Boston. Our patient census was down, so I had extra time to spend with the children. I would take Robbie out to the hospital garden. There, in pleasant weather, hospital staff and patients would congregate, eating their lunches or just taking in the sun. The azaleas that lined the walks were blossoming with a surplus of brilliant pinks, whites, and reds.

On some days, the hospital arranged to have entertainment in the garden for the children—clowns, singers, magicians. Robbie and I went to the garden one afternoon when a trio of musicians was playing. As I pushed his wheelchair out the door and onto the garden walk, Robbie grunted his displeasure with where I had stopped. He took hold of the wheels and pushed himself right up to the stringed bass player. Closer and closer he pressed, reaching out his stubby hand as though wanting to touch the music that thumped out. Robbie noticed everything, once picking up a discarded and crumpled cigarette package, holding it close to his face. For a long time he had examined the cellophane sparkling in the sunlight.

The day came when Robbie went to surgery for his heart. I was working the second shift, so he would be through surgery, I figured, by mid-afternoon when I came in. Cardiac surgery was so routine on our division that it never occurred to me that there might be a problem. When the elevator doors opened onto the floor, there stood Joan, the head nurse. She had been waiting for me with the news that Robbie had died in surgery. She asked if I would like to go to the staff lounge for a while before coming onto the floor for work. I nodded gratefully.

In the lounge, Joan simply sat with me for a few minutes, saying how sorry she was and that she knew Robbie and I had become close. She then left, saying that I could go to work whenever I felt ready.

I worked through the afternoon in a kind of melancholy and detached haze. A quietness had settled over our division, an unspoken sympathy and grief. The staff treated each other with added gentleness. This always happened when one of our young patients died.

Later that evening, one of the medical residents came shuffling down the hall. I had gotten to know him somewhat through Robbie, who had been his patient. This young doctor, only a year or so older than I, wore his emotions with a refreshing openness. I stood idly just down the hall from the nurses' station. The doctor walked toward me, stopping close by and blankly examining a patient's chart. His heart clearly was not in it. He lowered the chart and stared gloomily into the floor. "I guess not many around here will miss Robbie," he said with a bitterness that took me off guard. Then he gave me a quick glance, shook his head slightly, and walked off, still looking at the floor.

He was right, I realized. To many people at the hospital, Robbie had been a "problem patient," a drain on an already overworked staff. Perhaps that young resident understood better than I that some regarded patients like Robbie as hardly worth the trouble, as medical "lost causes."

As days passed, I felt more and more deeply what a gift Robbie had been. I had learned much from him—the rewards of persisting in communication and friendship, making a connection with someone very different from myself. I learned to look more closely at things, to listen, to smell, to touch with greater care the world right around me. I had also begun to learn that those we set out to help very often end up being the ones who help and heal us.

A Handicapping World

After having known her for several years, I sit with her in my office. She called me, wanting to know if we could talk. As I hung up the phone, I felt grateful relief, for I knew that, given her life and its challenges, she must have the need to talk about things in more than a perfunctory way.

She is physically handicapped, the result of an automobile accident when she was in high school. A popular and active girl in school, her world had been turned upside down. The twenty years or so since the accident have been consumed by the work of physical recovery. She has strained for every inch of improvement in speech or mobility, challenged by physicians' doubts, pushing herself, proving everyone wrong. She *would* walk and talk again.

Far beyond others' expectations, she has gained back a great deal. She walks with only the aid of a cane, and increasingly without it. Her speech is slow and labored, but understandable. Anyone listening with the attentiveness we should give each other anyway would be able to understand her. She continues to live with a discipline and focus foreign to most of us. Still pushing, she plans a great deal for her life.

But now she wants to talk. The inner story comes out, the story beneath the courageous fight, the physical struggle. "I feel like I've lost twenty years of my life," she says. "Everyone my age has been married, maybe has children. They have progressed in careers. They socialize easily."

After talking together for nearly an hour, the deepest-lying issue presents itself—loneliness. She feels lonely at home, yet lonely in crowds, as well. People perceive her as "special," her disability being the main thing they notice. She thinks of herself as attractive, which she is. And yet, people reflect back to her an image of herself as unappealing. No matter how hard others try to be sensitive to her, to relate in a nonpatronizing way, she still feels that she is treated with kid gloves, and that, at bottom, people would rather not be with her if they had the choice. She is afraid of what she might do in public, stumble or drop something. Because her speech is slow, some people assume she is mentally retarded. Yet, she holds a hard-won degree in library science.

"I used to think that slow was good," she said, with a slight chuckle. Her remarkable strength has been that she has come to see the catastrophe in her life as a teacher, not just an obstacle to be overcome. Being "slowed down" makes us careful and attentive, when the momentum of contemporary life makes us rush through our days without really seeing, or touching, or learning. But now she faces indignities from well-meaning people at work who ask her to do some task, only to end up doing it themselves out of their impatience. Persons who are "slow" have much to teach us. As we worship speed and efficiency, how inhuman and desultory our lives become! Are we not the ones who are truly disabled?

Throughout our talk I realized afresh how much we build self-esteem on the sandy soil of others' opinions of us. If our sense of self-worth comes from outside ourselves, it is fragile indeed. In a society that tells us our "image" is so important, an image that must be created by the right clothes, the right car, the right "look," we risk being like brightly adorned but empty shells. My friend has fought a great inner battle to find the true foundation of self-worth. For the moment, she had lost sight of this.

Toward the end of our time together, something in me begged to be expressed. You are not the problem, I said. You live, we all live, in a sick and misled society and world that see only the physical and apparent, not the underlying and deep realities of persons. You must keep reminding yourself that those who are uncomfortable with you, who cannot or will not know the whole of you, are the ones who are confused and lost. You must continue to be who you are, without shame. Whether or not people are comfortable with that is not your problem, ultimately.

We agreed to continue to meet. As she left, I felt a heavy sadness, not for her but for a world of confused values, a world that makes it so hard for us to stay focused on what truly matters. At the same time, I felt hopeful because of her courage and the truth of her life. I thought again, as I have so often, how fortunate I am when people share their struggles with me. They are my teachers. It had certainly been so that day.

Finally, beloved, whatever is true, whatever is honorable, whatever is just, whatever is pure, whatever is pleasing, whatever is commendable, if there is any excellence and if there is anything worthy of praise, think about these things…and the God of peace will be with you.

Philippians 4:8, 9c

People-pleasing and People-serving

Am I now seeking human approval, or God's
approval? Or am I trying to please people? If I were
still pleasing people, I would not be a servant of
Christ.

Galatians 1:10

Each of us must please our neighbor for the good
purpose of building up the neighbor. For Christ
did not please himself....

Romans 15:2–3a

As far as we know, the same person probably wrote both these passages! How can it be that Paul can at one point reject the idea of trying to please people, and at another enjoin his brothers and sisters in faith to please others? Is Paul writing out of both sides of his mouth? Or perhaps there is more to be learned here.

People-pleasing is a very common motivation among us. Parents, with every good intention, impress upon their children the importance of "being good" so that others will like them, so that they will find acceptance and approval. In the southern United States, a high premium is placed on "niceness." "Nice" is probably the loftiest adjective that can be used in describing another person. In fact, when we scratch the surface of much American Christianity, what it means to be a Christian often boils down to whether or not a person is "nice"— courteous, fair, responsible, likable, certainly not a "troublemaker!"

People-pleasing is not completely a bad thing. Treating others with respect and courtesy, making them feel comfortable and showing them kindness—these are not unimportant matters. However, there are problems with people-pleasing. The assumption works its way into our psyche that we can and are to make people happy. And if they are not happy, especially about something we say or do or are, we feel that we have failed.

I remember a young man I knew years ago who was chained to his mother's expectations that he become a priest. He felt so torn between his compulsion to please his mother and his own desires for his life that he would periodically experience very real convulsions. In varying degrees, we suffer unnecessarily out of our compulsions to please others. We abandon our own lives, short-circuit our own feelings, and generally muddle up life for ourselves and others.

A preoccupation with pleasing others keeps us from the truth of our own lives, diverts our energies from what we are called to be and to do within our own uniqueness. I am not persuaded that Jesus' call to lose ourselves, to die to ourselves, meant in any way creating some sort of vacuum where the self should be.

Paul was trying to explain to some very contentious early Christians that his work had a deeper purpose than making them happy. No doubt, Paul's ego must have been stung by accusations that were thrown at him, challenges to his integrity, swipes at his reputation. Pleasing God, however, was his vocation, and theirs, as well. And pleasing God is much different from pleasing people, for it means responding fully and joyously to God's life-giving love and truth. Belonging first to God grants us true selfhood, the God-created self. Believing that we can or ought to please each other, we abdicate our divine birthright and the freedom that comes from it.

Now we can understand why Paul could say on other occasions that we are precisely to please others. This kind of pleasing has to do with serving one another in the love of God. And this, not from a position of psychological, emotional, or spiritual debility, but expressly out of the grace of God's love and truth in our own lives.

If we have avoided finding our own lives in God, then the commands of God to love and serve others become chaffing yokes around our souls. Unfortunately, many Christians feel constrained to love others but experience, instead of joy and freedom, resentfulness and unhappiness. While not taking away his command to love others, Jesus at the same time calls us to find our lives in God's being and love, which are the same. Then we can abandon our fruitless efforts to please people and discover the truly fulfilling way of joyful service, "pleasing our neighbor for the good purpose of building up the neighbor."

From Victim to Witness

"No one takes [my life] from me, but I lay it down
of my own accord. I have power to lay it down,
and I have power to take it up again."

John 10:18

Christian faith is full of "dynamite" teachings. The word *dynamite* comes from the Greek word *dunamis,* which means "power," particularly the power that comes from God. This kind of power can either make our lives full of new meaning and purpose, or, if handled carelessly, can "blow up in our faces."

Jesus' teachings are laced with "dynamite" ideas such as humility, service to others, losing our lives. Christian life can take these "dynamite" words and ideas and become completely unhappy, even neurotic. The kind of self-denial about which Jesus speaks can turn into a psychological and emotional program for our own mental and spiritual illness, if not handled with reflection, prayer, and a growing wisdom.

Jesus speaks to the Pharisees about the good shepherd who lays down his life for the sheep. Jesus, as the Good Shepherd, has God's love because he lays down his life in order to take it up again. John, the Gospel writer, is speaking from the vantage point of the resurrection: Jesus laid down his life (crucifixion) and picked it up again (resurrection). The important point here is that "no one makes" Jesus do this. He is not under a psychological compulsion. Jesus is not living out of a neurotic "martyr complex." The spiritual position of Jesus is one of strength, spiritual strength in knowing where he has come from and where he is going" (John 13:3). His actions and life are rooted in God. No one takes his life from him. It is freely given. Jesus is not a *victim*. He *is* a martyr, in the true sense of the Greek word *marturios,* a "witness" to something beyond himself.

Being a follower of Jesus does not mean making ourselves victims. Carrying our crosses does not mean slogging through life feeling persecuted. Certainly there are circumstances in our lives that "victimize" us. Some are fairly trivial, but build up in us a feeling of being "put upon." Other circumstances are acutely painful and threaten to incapacitate us. There are those in the world who are truly "victimized" by political or economic oppression, or by the devastation of natural disaster. Being a "victim" is not an uncommon human experience.

What interests me, however, are those people who experience victimizing circumstances but do not act like victims. There may well be a period of intense emotional stress, even shock. "I can't believe this has happened to me!" When cancer strikes or there is the sudden death of a loved one, we feel shock at the radical and painful change in our lives. However, if the "I can't believe this happened to me" response persists, we do continue to feel like victims. Out of our pain we deny what has happened, look for someone or something to blame, and feel powerless to do anything about our situation.

As we move from victimization to authentic grief, realizing and working through our loss, then we begin to leave the mentality, or spirituality, of the victim. We are *doing* something about our situation. We begin to realize that, though we can't control or change what has happened, we can meet it and work with the change that has been brought into our lives.

Being a victim means seeing ourselves at the mercy of life. We feel helpless and act as though we have no power. Our spirits gradually give up hope. My friend, whom I mentioned previously, was certainly the victim of a car accident that changed her life radically. However, she did not become a victim. Though with more deep-felt agony and struggle than anyone could be aware of, she began to make decisions about her life. She became a witness, one whose life of struggle speaks to others about meaning, purpose, courage, and, in terms of her faith, God's presence with us in suffering to bring new life.

When I think about this business of struggle and being victimized by life, I remember a pastoral visit I made many years ago. William and Sarah lived down the road from the church I served in the horse and tobacco country of central Kentucky. An aged couple, they showed in their bodies and faces the marks of a lifetime of hard physical work. Their home was a small shack of a house that looked very much like themselves—worn, bent, sagging. William and Sarah were not absolutely poor, and probably could have lived a bit better elsewhere. But they were part of that house and it was part of them.

As I visited them one day, they talked to me about their lives. "One day," William recalled, "we planted four acres of tobacco." Sarah had done it carrying her young child on her hip. Having cut and housed tobacco while I was in seminary, I knew just how big four acres could be. "That night," William continued, "a storm came through, washed away the whole thing." What did you do then, I asked? Sarah said matter-of-factly, "Well, the next day we planted it all again." There was no hint of self-pity or heroism. They simply did what they had to do.

I remember that story and those people whenever I realize again that there are hard moments in our lives when we have to start all over. Somehow we find the strength to do it. Somehow there is always room for us to decide what we will make of our lives, as shattered as they may be or seem. We are free to turn our lives from victim to witness.

The Courage of Aging

One morning, a phone call informed me that Mrs.— was at the hospital emergency room. She is in her eighties and lives alone. Like so many older persons, Mrs.— walks that precarious line between waning independence and waxing dependency. At two in the morning, she had fallen while getting out of bed. Later I learned that she had laid on the floor until she was found by her landlady at seven in the morning.

Arriving at the emergency room, I found Mrs.— lying on a gurney by the nurses' station. She was smiling warmly as ever, greeting me with a shy shake of her head as if to apologize for inconveniencing me. Already she was being discharged to go home, having only a slightly cracked rib. I pulled my car around to the hospital entrance and took her home.

The second-story apartment in which Mrs.— lived now loomed as a formidable escarpment. She shuffled slowly from the car to the front door, then managed the steps with great effort and many pauses for rest. When we finally entered her living room, I helped her get settled on the sofa, spreading an afghan over her legs. We talked a while as I put together in my mind the things I needed to do.

As we talked, she explained what had happened. The apartment being quite chilly—it was January—Mrs.— had managed to drag herself to the living room where there was an electric heater. She turned it on and covered herself with the very afghan that now lay across her legs. The phone was out of reach, so she waited through those long hours for someone to find her.

Settled down somewhat now, Mrs.— became more reflective, gazing out the window. Half to me and half to the gray January day, she said, "I guess I'm just not any good to anyone now."

How often I've heard those words, expressing the despondency of persons entering their final years alone. Their worlds begin to shrink with each fall, each illness, each limitation that sets in. Their circles of activities become smaller and smaller. The love of independence turns into the chilling recognition that they are becoming dependent. Mrs.—, whose drive to remain self-sufficient has been a great source of her vitality, is now facing an immovable reality. Like a stream encountering a barrier, her life must now carve out another channel. How difficult this transition is for her and all who share her circumstances. She will need support and care.

A few days later, I went back to check on Mrs.—. Several church members had lined up to visit her and bring food, checking on her by phone, as well. There is no undervaluing the ministry of the church to its older members!

She was not doing well, complaining of persistent weakness. I agreed to make an appointment for her with her doctor. Having done this, I left, promising to return that afternoon in time to take her to the doctor's office. When I returned, however, Mrs.—'s condition had deteriorated even more. She rose to go with me, but could not stand without support. Finally she quit her efforts and said that she simply couldn't make it. I helped her back to her chair and called the doctor again to explain the situation. He recommended that I call an ambulance to take Mrs.— to the hospital.

As we waited for the ambulance, we talked. She spoke of the morning she had fallen, and of the two emergency medical workers who had come with the ambulance. One of them had been a child when she worked at the city library. He would come in and she would help him choose books. How good it had been to see him, now a fine, bright, hardworking young man!

At last the ambulance arrived. And with it the same fellows! I was delighted to meet this young man and see that all she had said about him was true. He handled Mrs.— with gentleness and sensitivity. He was not patronizing in the least, and showed genuine interest in her. He even remembered that Mrs.— had a new great-grandchild.

After Mrs.— was settled in the hospital, I reminded her of her former words about her worthlessness. It seemed to me, I suggested, that she had certainly had something to do with this remarkably able and caring young man. She gave a slight but wonderful smile, indicating that she wasn't going to argue the point.

The stream of Mrs.—'s life was turning quickly. She would no longer live alone, but with her children. She would be leaving this town that had been her life for so many years—her work, the raising of her children, her life with her husband until his death. In the hospital, she talked about all of this, her voice weakened by her condition and a certain sadness. Yet, there was also emerging in her voice a soft and calm tone of acceptance. I realized that indeed she had been preparing for this moment, perhaps for a long time, within the solitude of her own spirit.

The day before Mrs.— left, I visited her in the hospital, our last visit. We talked for a while, holding hands. Then a prayer and an embrace. I walked out of the hospital into the cold sunlight of the January day. I realized how much I would miss this person who had been a friend as well as a parishioner.

That day I understood afresh that there are some things we must each face on our own, even though we don't face them alone. We can't take away from each other what we each will inevitably confront in our own lives, like our aging. We can only—and this is a big "only"—lift each other to God and to the unique journeys we all make. In this, there is certainly a loneliness. Yet we also find, with a certainty that cannot be grasped beforehand, an ultimate peace rooted in the deepest part of ourselves and in God.

Walking to my car that afternoon, I thought about the courage of Mrs.—, a courage that wasn't without fear, and therefore true courage. I prayed that I would find that courage in similar moments and circumstances.

> Even though I walk through the darkest valley,
>   I fear no evil;
> for you are with me….
>
> Psalm 23:4a

Weeds in the Garden

> "Let both of them grow together until
> the harvest…."
>
> Matthew 13:30a

Like many young boys, I earned spending money—spent all too soon, of course!—mowing neighbors' lawns in the spring and summer months. Often, before I set to work, my employer of the moment would survey the lawn with me, pointing out delicate, flowered areas that were to be carefully avoided. I normally listened with vague attentiveness, seeing this as pretty much a waste of time. I knew the difference between weeds and flowers! Actually, my botanical knowledge was miserably limited, and many times I would stand perplexed before a disputed plot of ground: Are those flowers or weeds? Being either too lazy or too proud, or both, to ask, I would plunge ahead, foregoing all doubt. Consequently my batting—or mowing—average was not very good. Most of the time I got the flowers, hoping afterwards my employer would not notice the error.

Jesus told a parable of weeds growing in the wheat field. The servants, seeing the weeds, ran to the master with the news. Now these were very philosophical servants. How did the weeds (evil) get there? They wanted to know the origins of things. Why is there evil in the world, in the first place? Where did it come from? The only answer their master offered was that "an enemy has done this." Just who the enemy was or why the foe should perpetrate such mischief are not addressed. This parable is unsatisfactory if we expect it to dish up a quick and easy answer to such big questions. But such is the nature of Jesus' parables—they furnish more questions, perhaps, than answers.

The presence of evil in the world, or in the church, for that matter, not to mention the evil in ourselves, is simply confirmed by the story. The biblical view of the world is not a rosy one that allows us to expect the world to be other than the curious, often painful, mixture of good and evil we find it to be.

The servants, however, continue. "Let's go out there and pull up those weeds!" These are not only philosophical servants; they are also eager, activist servants. They want to *do* something about the weeds, the evil. The master, though, says no. And here lies the surprising and challenging wisdom of the story.

Jesus, in this simple tale, counsels against zealous frontal attacks on evil. He has the master tell the servants to let the weeds grow right along with the wheat until the harvest. At that time, both the weeds and the wheat will be scythed. Then the weeds will be thrown out and destroyed. The wheat will be gathered into barns (God's kingdom).

It would appear that Jesus does not know much about modern farming or gardening. How unthinkable to let the weeds alone! But then Jesus was not giving gardening tips.

A subtle, yet essential part of this story is that the weed mentioned is of a particular sort, called "darnel." This weed looks very much like wheat, so much so that it was difficult for a person to tell the two apart. To make matters more complicated, the roots of the darnel become intertwined with wheat roots. The zealous servants might go wading into the wheatfield, grabbing up the weeds, or what they think are such, and end up destroying much of the wheat in their haste.

Certainly evil exists in the world, in the church, and in ourselves. Jesus was not indifferent to evil. But there is a cautionary word here. Jesus seems to know our penchant for zealous crusades for the causes we think "right." So, we come back to my problems as a young lawn mowing entrepreneur. Like the servants, I was not always able to distinguish flowers from weeds. When we take it upon ourselves to destroy evil, we can easily become evil ourselves, committing evil in the name of good. The witnesses to such activity are legion: shameful and bloody inquisitions; the burning of heretics; fragmented churches, each claiming to be the "right" one while condemning the rest. We have the later writings of such a theological giant as Martin Luther, in which he urged suppression of peasants by violence and spewed venomous epithets upon Jews. McCarthyism in the U.S. in the 1950s took a wide swath at perceived evil, claiming countless innocent victims. The suffering of peoples in so-called "Third World" countries has been intensified greatly by our own nation's policies that have supported many oppressive regimes simply because they expressed opposition to communism or socialism.

What are we to do? Are we to be passive, untroubled by the presence of real evil? Does Jesus remove from us the responsibility of confronting evil? No. Jesus, it is true, places his "no" in front of our crusading impulses, our weed-centered living. There is, however, a clear focus in the parable of the good seed. Was the seed you sowed, asked the servants, not good seed? The assumed answer is "yes." What was planted in the field was good seed. Here is a call to trust the master, that he has, indeed, sown the right stuff.

The master may well represent God, and if so, then the parable reaffirms the trustworthiness of God both as the source of good and the sovereign of life. A prominent, resounding theme of faith, found in the Psalms, is: "O give thanks to the Lord, for God is good; God's steadfast love endures forever."

In the end, the parable suggests at least two interpretations. The first has to do with our narrowness of vision when it comes to dealing with evil, that we are ill-equipped to decide ultimately what is and what is not evil. While being concerned with discerning what is evil, we need, at the same time, to recognize the relativity of our vision.

A second interpretation may lie along the lines of Jesus' teachings on nonresistance, nonconfrontation with regard to evil. Inherent in the parable is a call to wheat-centered living as a response to evil, overcoming evil with good. In the end, the most powerful response to evil consists of a life focused on the things that build up the good.

> Therefore, my beloved, be steadfast, immovable, always excelling in the work of the Lord, because you know that in the Lord your labor is not in vain.
>
> 1 Corinthians 15:58

This parable announces the sovereignty of God over good *and* evil. The ultimate fate of evil rests in God's hands, not ours, and has been decided already. This story of God's reign proclaims that evil, whatever its origin or appearance, ultimately has no future at all.

The Fly Rod and the Seine Net

"Again, the kingdom of heaven is like a net that was
thrown into the sea and caught fish of every kind;
when it was full, they drew it ashore, sat down, and
put the good into baskets but threw out the bad. So
it will be at the end of the age."

Matthew 13:47–49a

Since the appearance of the movie *A River Runs Through It*,
there has been a great boom in fly-fishing. As a result, the fly-
fishing industry has done very well. Yes, even I caught the bug.
My father and I fly-fished when I was young. I remember being
fascinated with the long, flowing casts, and enjoyed navigating
by foot the currents of many a trout stream. Maybe part of the
attraction of the sport is that it gives grown men permission to
do what they loved as kids—wading around in water!

Fly-fishing is precise, not like lounging on a riverbank with
a worm on your hook, waiting for any old fish to bite. Just the
right rod, with just the right line, with just the right fly...all
aimed at getting just the right fish, a wily and hypersensitive
trout! But there's more. These days, fashion seems of consum-
mate importance, so...just the right waders, the right vest, the
right landing net, and certainly the right hat. Fly-fishing is very
precise, and fashion-conscious!

Water and fishing figure prominently in the Gospels. Jesus
calls some disciples away from one kind of fishing to another—
from fish to people. After the resurrection, Jesus reveals himself
when he instructs the disciples to put their nets out on the opposite side of the boat. Before, they weren't catching a thing.

Now their nets are filled to bursting. And Jesus shares a fish breakfast—a kind of fish and bread eucharist—with the disciples on the beach after their big catch (John 21).

Jesus uses fishing to describe the realm of God, how that realm works, how it will look when it dawns. The realm of God is like a seine net thrown out broadly into the sea. As it is drawn through the water to the boat, it scoops up every kind of fish. Then the fisherfolk separate out the "keepers" and throw the rest away. That's like God's realm, says Jesus. At the end of the age, the angels will come and separate out the "keepers" (the righteous, the faithful) from the rest, whose fate is described in fiery terms.

We may want to zero in on that last part, either captivated by the "bad" folks getting their just desserts, or troubled by the stern biblical images. But the parable doesn't let us focus there. It is very clear about where our concern should be—not the judgment, but the fishing. God throws out the seine net broadly, through the witness and work of the church. Our fishing, our bearing witness to the outreaching love of God, is to be broad and indiscriminate. Ours is not to decide who is or is not worthy, who is acceptable and who is not, who will benefit the church and who might bring in "questionable" elements. The church through the centuries has perpetuated much harm by such selective parceling out of the good news of God's love. Race, culture, lifestyle, beliefs—so many human variables have been used to narrow the door to God's realm.

The parable teaches us an important wisdom. It is not fly-fishing but seine net fishing that comprises the ministry of God's love through the church. When we seek only the right kind of fish (our kind of folks!), it is not the gospel we proclaim but the ethos of our particular group. We serve God's realm, God's new order, best when we pick up, not our fly rods, but the seine net of God's expansive love and grace. And we do our best fishing when we remember that sorting out is not our work but God's.

If the church can grow in the wisdom of this little but all-important parable, then we would be surprised at how exciting it is when all sorts of people are drawn to the warmth and light of God's love. When we reach out to all people, we find that the differences they bring turn into manifold gifts for the work of the church as it proclaims God's outreaching love.

As a Little Child

"Truly I tell you, whoever does not receive the kingdom of God as a little child will never enter it."

Mark 10:15

"...but she out of her poverty has put in everything she had, all she had to live on."

Mark 12:44

In the summer of 1984, my wife and I were given by our congregation the gift of a three-week trip to what was then East and West Germany. We traveled as part of a small group of pastors, theologians, and students, sharing an interest in the church resistance to the Hitler regime. Particularly our journey focused on the life of the pastor/theologian Dietrich Bonhoeffer. Bonhoeffer had been part of the failed assassination attempt in June 1944 against Hitler. He was executed at Flossenburg concentration camp in April 1945, only a few days before the camp was liberated.

One morning we gathered outside the Hotel Elephant in the town of Weimar, East Germany. The previous day we had explored the museums, shops, and streets of this famous center of the arts in German culture. Weimar—the creative home of Schiller and Goethe, and so many other artists and musicians!

This day, however, we were to take a markedly different tour—Buchenwald concentration camp, which was only a short distance outside the town. What irony! This town so celebrative of the human creative spirit and of the beauty of life, and yet, just moments away, one of the sites of the most degraded and evil manifestations of the human spirit.

We milled about the fountain in the town square, waiting for the whole group to assemble. A dull sunlight barely held on before what was becoming a dreary and overcast sky, suited better, I suppose, to our impending pilgrimage.

As we waited and talked, we noticed a delightful young girl, about seven or eight years old, standing at the fountain. She had Down's syndrome. We all felt drawn to her. She was unwrapping a chocolate bar, preparing to enjoy it. Unable to speak her language, we set about finding little ways of making contact. Soon we were all throwing our eyes wide at her candy bar, rubbing our stomachs, and passing our tongues over our lips. For us, it was all in fun. However, this little girl, this bundle of sunshine on a gloomy day, suddenly did something that caught us completely off our guard. She began to unwrap the whole of her chocolate bar. It became obvious that she was intending to share her candy with us, not just a bit but the whole thing! We rapidly reversed our gestures, smiling, shaking our heads, and thrusting our hands forward, trying to say, "Oh no, please! We were only joking with you!" Finally she got our meaning, smiled slightly, and went back to what she was doing before these silly Americans entered the picture!

After this bright encounter and our tour of Buchenwald, my mind and heart were filled with reflections. Forty years earlier, the brothers and sisters of that Down's syndrome girl had been systematically mutilated by "scientific experiments" and murdered in mobile extermination units. Mentally and physically disabled children and adults were the first to go into the Nazi machinery of death. They were among the millions who had been judged less than human, *lebensunwerten Lebens*, "life unworthy of life." The Nazi period stands as a grim reminder of what can happen when human diversity is assaulted and we strive toward an idealized sameness, a movement that contains in it the seeds of violence.

There are so many urgent lessons to learn from the Nazi period. One such lesson is that we need always to be vigilant for trends in our society, our world, and in our own hearts toward deciding the worth of other human beings, questioning whether or not certain persons or groups should have rights, respect, or understanding. Calculating who is and is not of worth is a dangerous and insidious human cruelty.

Nazi Germany and the Holocaust, along with other events of human evil, give rise to an important sense of shame. They remind us of our capacities for evil and violence. Such events may even bring our spirits to the brink of cynicism and hopelessness about our own humanity.

However, when I remember that little girl at the fountain in Weimar, I feel another kind of shame. I am stirred by what I am not yet, but hope to become. Her astounding and quick generosity, her desire to share with us every bit of something precious to her, spoke of what is best in us as human beings. She stood in the graying light of that morning as a bright ray of truth and therefore hope, against the dismal backdrop of what lay at the outskirts of that town, a monument to what is the worst in us.

We are capable of much evil, but also much good. In our hearts are the seeds of fear and prejudice, but also of compassionate community. Our lives are a struggle to overcome the one by allowing the other to grow in us and transform us and our world. This very struggle is part of our dignity as human beings. The struggle is difficult, but not hopeless. It is, in fact, charged with hope, because God is in our struggles to be fully human.

[This meditation was written for the National Conference of Christians and Jews, which presented to Kaye and me the Brotherhood/Sisterhood Citation, June 1994.]

Not "Just" a Duck!

On the glorious splendor of your majesty,
and on your wondrous works, I will meditate.

Psalm 145:5

Periodically I go on retreat at the Motherhouse of the Sisters of Loretto, in Kentucky. My wife and I have friends of longstanding in that community of vowed sisters, and their ecumenical spirit always makes us feel at home in their community.

The Motherhouse was established in April 1812 by the Rev. Charles Nerinckx, a Roman Catholic priest. He was a native of Belgium who had fled his homeland because of religious persecution. He came to Baltimore, then was sent into Kentucky, working there with compulsive vigor to establish churches. There he also established the Sisters of Loretto as a teaching order. Today, the sisters are engaged in a variety of work—teaching, social work, nursing, community organizing, and much more.

The Loretto Motherhouse consists of a church and various other buildings that have kept their historic beauty while changing from time to time to meet the shifting needs and purposes of the community. In former days, income for the order was generated partially by the farm that was worked by the sisters themselves. Eventually, however, the farm was leased to neighboring farmers when the work of the community was directed elsewhere. The farmland on which the Motherhouse sits provides a gentle pastoral environment for guests who come for spiritual refreshment and direction.

I have been fortunate to find hospitality in such places as Loretto. Protestants, in general, have not been given to spiritual retreats, much less silence! We are a very wordy and social strain of Christianity! For myself, however, I have found it essential to my professional life as well as my personal existence to make retreats regularly, reorienting my mind and life. To belong to God and others, as we are taught by Christ, is not an easy road in this world. We become too full of anxiousness and burdens to function lovingly and in faithful and free ways. Our spirits are quickly emptied of God's Spirit as we live in our frantic and troubled world. Times of withdrawal, as Jesus himself seemed to have taken from the hints we get in the Gospels, offer a re-centering of our lives. Whether for a week, or for even a day spent walking in the woods, or for an hour devoted to silence, retreats are opportunities to let our lives ripen under the warmth and light of God's love.

On the last day of one of my retreats at Loretto, I took a farewell stroll through the farm and up to Mary's Lake, one of two on the back part of the property. The crunching of my feet on the gravel path that led by the barns aroused the half-interested gazes of the cows.

Normally when I took my walks to the lake, I would find no one there, since my retreat took place in winter, not the most popular time. But now, as I rose on the crest of the bank, I saw something large and white out of the corner of my eye. What was it? Some exotic creature? A heron, perhaps? Or maybe a Canadian goose? When I looked full at it, my mind said immediately, "Oh, it's just a duck!" Yes, it was a duck, just a normal, everyday duck. However, I reflected on what it meant that my mind said "just" a duck.

There stood the creature on the edge of the lake opposite me, stock-still and marble white. The animal seemed surprisingly large, standing erect and surveying the whole scene in a magisterial way. I quietly took a seat by the lake, and watched. Only at long intervals would the duck dip its beak into the water for a morsel of whatever food a duck gleans from the water's edge. Then it would resume its regal posture and its absolute stillness. After a long while, I stood and walked back to the buildings of the Motherhouse, bringing my retreat to a close.

Duck. Such a bland name for so marvelous a creature! I had been so used to seeing ducks that I seldom, if ever, really *saw* them. I realized that this was the purpose of a retreat, after all, to awaken one's vision and spirits so that one notices, truly notices what is going on in and around oneself. There, at the end of my retreat, I thought to myself—how does one know if one's retreat has been successful? The answer: When a duck is no longer "just" a duck.

When we see as we were created to see, we catch glimpses of glory all around us. A duck is no longer "just" a duck. A leaf is no longer "just" a leaf. A wife or husband is no longer "just" a wife or husband. A friend is no longer "just" a friend. Each day is no longer "just" another day. And we ourselves are no longer "just" ourselves.

And the one who was seated upon the throne said, "See, I am making all things new."

Revelation 21:5